DATE DUE

AUG 0 5 2000		
AG 5 '00		
~~AG 20 00~~		
NO 22 '02		
AP 10 03		
NO 20 03		
DE 1 04		
DE 17 04		
AR 31 05		
OC 5 05		
DE 6 05		

DEMCO 38-296

ALTERNATIVE SENTENCING

Electronically Monitored Correctional Supervision

Richard Enos
Clifford M. Black
James F. Quinn
John E. Holman

Wyndham Hall Press

ALTERNATIVE SENTENCING:
Electonically Monitored Correctional Supervision

Richard Enos, D.S.W.
Clifford M. Black, Ph.D.
James F. Quinn, Ph.D.
John E. Holman, Ph.D.

Wyndham Hall Press is an academic imprint
of the Cloverdale Corporation.

Library of Congress Catalog Card Number

92-050697

ISBN 1-55605-218-9 (paperback)
ISBN 1-55605-219-7 (hardback)

Cloverdale Corporation
Bristol, IN 46507-9460

Written

By

Richard Enos, D.S.W.
Professor of Sociology and Social Work
Director, Center for Public Service
University of North Texas

Clifford M. Black, Ph.D.
Professor of Sociology and Criminal Justice
Dean, School of Education and Arts and Sciences
Laredo State University

James F. Quinn, Ph.D.
Assistant Professor of Criminal Justice
Institute of Criminal Justice
University of North Texas

John E. Holman, Ph.D.
Associate Professor of Criminal Justice
Director, Institute of Criminal Justice
University of North Texas

TABLE OF CONTENTS

CHAPTER 7: A STUDY OF THE EFFECTS OF ELECTRONICALLY
            MONITORED HOME CONFINEMENT ON OFFENDERS
            AND THEIR HOME ENVIRONMENTS: METHODOLO-
            GY, INSTRUMENTATION, AND DEMOGRAPHY

CHAPTER 8: AN ANALYSIS OF THE DATA CONCERNING THE
            EFFECTS OF ELECTRONICALLY MONITORED HOME
            CONFINEMENT ON OFFENDERS AND THEIR HOME
            ENVIRONMENTS

CHAPTER 9: CRITICAL ISSUES IN THE FUTURE FOR ELECTRONIC MONITORING PROGRAMS

CHAPTER 1

THE HISTORY OF PROBATION

INTRODUCTION

A treatment of the history of probation almost necessitates a discussion of the definition of the practice and a location of accountability for it. Essentially, probation refers to a process in which an offender is assigned to one or more forms of community supervision as an alternative to imprisonment in some governmental or private facility.[1] Perhaps the most helpful summation of the practice is provided by the translation of the term from its roots in Latin, which reflect the ideas of testing, proving and forgiving. In other words, probation provides an opportunity for an offender to "prove" that he or she is capable of remaining in the community, in spite of the fact that he or she has been found guilty of a crime. It offers a second chance for the community to "test" or determine whether the individual will or can obey the laws of society. A fuller definition and one of a more legal nature would designate probation as a method of responding to crimes of a less serious nature, misdemeanors and minor felonies, and frequently, first offenses, in which the judgement rendered is a suspended sentence. The offender is assigned to the supervision of a probation officer for a specified period of time and as long as laws and probation rules are obeyed. In the event of a violation of laws or rules of probation, the original sentence or other sanctions can be reimposed on the offender.[2]

There are at least three components of the practice which need to be underscored. First, the release is conditional. Second, assuming that all conditions are fulfilled, the penalty will be served in the community. Third, the practice includes supervision. These components of probation are included as essential elements in the definition of probation used by the American Bar Association.[3] Often a sentencing judge will impose a prison term on an offender but suspends the execution of it and places the offender on probation. Thus, with respect to the second component, the offender does not spend time in prison unless conditions prescribed by the court are violated.

PROBATION VERSUS PAROLE

In defining probation it is helpful to compare the concept with the practice of parole. The latter can be contrasted with probation in that the offender has been incarcerated prior to release, whereas probation is a penalty rendered by a judge rather than some form of imprisonment or a jail sentence. A second contrast occurs with respect to the location of the decision for release into the community. The release of the offender into the community, on probation, is the result of a decision made in the judicial system. The decision to return an offender to the community, on parole, is a direct result of a decision made in the correctional organization.[4]

Although this differentiation of parole and probation seems quite distinct when the two practices are contrasted, serious differences do exist with respect to accountability or location of authority for the programs. In essence, the dichotomy outlined is, in theory, correct. However, in practice, it requires some qualifications even though it is the courts which supervise the probation process. Bowker[1] contends that probation is really part of the corrections mechanism. He bases his contention on the fact that the sentence occurs after a finding of guilt. Thus, logically, it becomes a part of the corrections function. The most pragmatic view is that it is more important to understand the reality of how probation is administered than to understand the organizational part of the criminal justice system in which it is located. In short, politically speaking, the function of probation may be more important than its structural or organizational location. However, in most states, it refers to a set of procedures supervised by the judiciary in the local community.

The importance of this discussion has to do not only with defining probation but also with understanding the actual locus of control for these programs; especially, when considering alternative approaches or innovations in the practice, the impact of the programs on offenders and the quality or effectiveness of the programs. Although state correctional structures may, in fact, be formally responsible for probation services, locally elected judges may for all practical purposes be in charge. This has been an ongoing controversy and has significance not only with respect to corrections reform, but also regarding the lack of appropriate training of judges in corrections and the additional burdening of an overcrowded court system. Some criminal justice professionals and theoreticians argue, in fact, that judges are not trained in the area of corrections and that such programs add significant and unnecessary responsibilities to already overloaded courts. Other participants in the debate underscore the increased stigma for offenders if the program is located in corrections as opposed to the judiciary. Specifically, this perspective contends that identification of probation programs with correctional organizations would create an unnecessary and significant stigma for the offender.[3,4]

One of the arguments for including probation as a part of the correctional component of criminal justice is the fact that other human service agencies used by probation are a part of the "executive branch" of government. Thus, some criminal justice practitioners and criminologists argue that probation officers have more direct access to such services if the probation officers themselves are a part of the corrections organizations. Further, it is posited that the probability is higher that such services can, and will be, exploited to the greatest benefit of their clients. Those who support the concept of judicial control argue that the close relationship between the judge and the supervising officer is critical to the most constructive consequences of probation. Included in this perception is the idea that such a relationship between judges and probation officers engenders confidence in presentence reports and the supervision of cases. A corollary may also be that this system permits judges to appoint probation officers who will be more likely to reflect, and defer to, the community standards and political structures.[4]

In spite of such historic differentiations of probation and parole, some states and the federal government have adopted models for merging the two practices. Rationale for such models have often been more in terms of efficiency rather than in terms of philosophy and effectiveness. Still, there is considerable logic underlying such models and a strong philosophical argument could be made for this practice. However, as has been emphasized here, corrections professionals have made significant arguments for the specific administrative locations of both probation and parole. Unless the models which are used in merging the two practices are under the auspices of the probation departments and the courts, then, they are still subject to all of the criticisms outlined.

Thus, the differentiation of probation in theory and practice will be of critical importance throughout this book. This reflects the reality of current models and the politics with which each program must be concerned, but in this instance, particularly, the political issues with which probation departments must be involved. The issues which relate to that discussion will also be observed to have genuine impact on the use of electronic monitoring (EM) as one alternative in the probation process. Specifically, the actual control of the programs, the training of those administering them, and their perceived effects on offenders have tremendous impact on the responsibilities for introducing innovative techniques and the probabilities for the success of such programs. A treatment of the history of probation to the present time illustrates this fact and provides evidence for this assertion.

THE DEVELOPMENT OF PROBATION

The first practice of probation is usually dated as 1841 and is attributed to the efforts and actions of a wealthy Boston merchant, John Augustus. Edward Savage, a Boston police officer, is usually identified as the first official probation officer and is thought to have conducted the first presentence investigation.[5] Both probation and parole have evolved as a result of major social and legal reforms throughout Western nations in the Nineteenth century. In particular, the reforms represented attempts to provide more humane treatment than was provided by fixed punishments. Probation and parole may have been the most significant contributions to new developments in penology.

Although the specific practice is often identified with the activities of Augustus, there are other historical antecedents. Although scholars do not necessarily agree upon the importance, or direct correlation, between these antecedents and the current practice, most agree that precedents exist in various aspects of English Common Law.[6] Some scholars have pointed to the early practices of reprieves and pardons used in England as the forerunner of probation.[7] Specifically, these practices included benefit of clergy, judicial reprieve, and recognizance. One of the earliest practices which could have lent credence to initial attempts at probation was known as "benefit of clergy". The Church claimed sole authority over the behavior of members of the clergy. Thus, all clergy crimes were adjudicated by Church courts as opposed to criminal courts.[6] Another possible origin for probation is the suspended sentence. This was a practice which diverted offenders from prison. A second violation could lead to imprisonment.[8] Other scholars contend that such suspensions or judicial reprieves were not permanent. Rather they were used as temporary measures in circumstances such as an offender awaiting or seeking a pardon. In some cases judges resorted to such practices if they were dissatisfied with a verdict or requested additional or more specific information.[2] The practice of releasing offenders through recognizance involved the development of an agreement between the offender and the court in which the offender pledges to abide by certain behaviors, particularly obeying the law, and to follow specific procedures to insure that such violations would not occur again. Such specific procedures might involve agreeing to appear at specified times to provide assurance of appropriate behavior, a payment of a fine, or providing some form of a guarantee of monetary payment, or a bond, for any new violation or failure to appear.[2]

In assessing the historical precedents of probation, it is essential to emphasize that while these practices from English Common Law were influential in the development of this procedure in both England and the United States, in the latter they culminated in their own unique and historically significant variations. One example was "provisional filing" of cases in Massachusetts. This practice permitted the indefinite suspension of a guilty verdict after sentence was pronounced. The sufficient conditions for this practice included extenuating circumstances, such as situations in which higher courts were expected to render opinions on similar legal questions. Approval of both defendant and prosecutor were necessary prior to the rendering of this decision.[2] The critical historical fact with respect to these variations was a 1916 United States Supreme Court ruling which declared that these precedents did not provide grounds in Federal courts for indefinitely, or through these means, for permanently suspending a sentence. In fact, however, these innovations had gained considerable support and approval. When the innovations were themselves ruled illegal, this resulted in the passing of actual statutes authorizing probation and the suspension of a sentence. Thus, the decision by the Supreme Court to terminate practices which had emerged from English common law resulted in the creation of laws specifically permitting suspended sentences and probation.[5] Further, it is of significance in the discussion of the historical development of probation to emphasize that the first statute authorizing the practice in the United States was passed in Massachusetts in 1898. Such laws did not emerge in England until 1907.

Although the first case for which Augustus served as a probation officer involved an adult male, the practice did not receive widespread approval until it was used by the juvenile courts. In fact, few states had such laws for the supervision of probationers by 1900. In 1899, the first juvenile court was established. It was this development which led to dramatic increases in the use of probation. Current research indicates that, even now, probation is the most common disposition for cases officially processed through the juvenile courts.[9] By 1910, forty states used probation for juveniles and all states were using such programs by 1925. In contrast, it was thirty-one years later, or 1956, before all of the states had some form of adult probation.[1] Although the growth of adult probation was slower than the growth of juvenile probation, the outcomes were quite similar. For example, it has been hypothesized that as high as 60 percent of all offenders sentenced to correctional treatment are placed on probation.[8]

It should also be noted that the rapid growth of the use of probation for juveniles was later paralleled in adult probation. Records indicate that by 1924 perhaps as many as 200,000 offenders a year were being placed on probation. These figures themselves can be misleading with respect to the significance and use of probation. For example, for the figures for any year, when control is provided for the short-term nature of many probated sentences, the number of persons on parole during any one year increases dramatically.   Thus, the figures reported may indicate one million such individuals, when in fact, twice as many individuals may actually have been on probation at some time during that particular year.[1]

The overall impact of these data cannot be overemphasized.   That is, that the practice of probation is a significantly important mechanism in response to criminal offenders and continues to grow in importance.   That process and growth has not been without some transformation in the practice.   Further, there is evidence to suggest that recent changes or innovations are a direct result of the problematic nature of the program.   For example, in 1990 Clear and Cole (among others), discussed the fact that numerous states were experimenting with models for combining probation and parole.[10] In addition, although the concept of "community corrections" has its own history, one might well argue that the inclusion of a variety of supervisory and rehabilitative approaches under this concept clearly demonstrates the changing nature of the probation process.   The development of community corrections is definitely one of the most significant developments in the field of corrections. It certainly has had a major impact upon the practice of probation and parole. The fact that community corrections approaches developed within traditional probation programs without having been first created as a part of a definite philosophy may in fact explain the ambiguous or vague nature of the concept.

PROBLEMS AND ISSUES IN PROBATION

One of the most problematic aspects of probation concerns the appropriate caseload size or the average number of probationers assigned to individual probation officers.   Specifically, the concern has been about the optimal size of the caseloads. Exceedingly large caseloads are frequently cited as a significant problem with respect to: accomplishing the goals and objectives of probation; the inefficient use of resources; and the ineffective guidance of the offender. We are now at a point of a major crisis in the criminal justice system in this country because of the increase in the use of probation has been far more rapid than the training and employment of officers to supervise this process.   It is difficult to discuss what constitutes an ideal caseload since there is no unanimity in the field concerning this issue. While various ideal sizes have been posited, little empirical evidence has been provided to support such claims. Sizes of 35-50 are commonly proposed as ideal. [11] The ideal of the 50 person caseload was established by the National Probation Association. A Presidential Commission in 1967 proposed a 35 person caseload. Arguments for caseload sizes have been predicated upon the belief that individual differences among probationers create differential demands upon a probation officer's time and energy.[4]   Furthermore, the

American Correctional Association proposes a formula, but posits no specific caseload size. The criteria proposed by this association is "constant contact" by the officer, as opposed to any specific number of offenders to be supervised.[11]

Although Gettinger[11] correctly underscores the absence of empirical evidence supporting an "ideal" caseload size, Cole reports that there are examples of caseloads of 150 to 300 offenders.[3] In such situations, it is unlikely that the probation officer will be able to assist in providing many of the services needed by the offender. Yet, under these circumstances, supervision may be an impossible task as well. Considering the other expectations associated with the role of the probation officer, it is realistic to believe that it may become almost impossible for the officer to provide assistance and supervision to probationers. A variety of strategies or alternatives have been developed to respond to such situations. For example, situations exist in which the contact between offender and officer and for supervision by the officer are primarily accomplished by telephone or by mail status reports. This procedure has been more prevalent in urban areas than in other geographic settings. Under such circumstances, it can be argued that the goals of criminal sanctions with respect to the judicial sentence cannot be accomplished.

Most practitioners and criminologists seem to agree that there is a point at which the caseload reaches a size beyond which any attempt to accomplish the expectations of probation are useless and sanctions have no effect. In the most extreme view, the inability to provide appropriate supervision may well have rendered the practice useless as a social control mechanism. Recent reforms, such as changes in classification approaches, reevaluation of offender service needs, analyses of the probation experience, more advanced training of officers, and the onrush of many new private and community probation alternatives have alleviated, to some degree, the crises that had existed with respect to size of the caseload. A second, inter-related, and equally important consideration which contributes to the problematic nature of probation is recidivism. Statistical analysis suggests that success rates are not significantly higher than those for incarceration, except for offenders on felony probation. An idealist might suggest that even though the differences between incarceration and probation with respect to the issue of recidivism are marginal, one might want to opt for probation because it is a more humane remedy. All things being equal, the rise in the use of probation is more precisely attributable to its lower costs. And, as a consequence, we have seen the devastating impact when unsupervised felony probationers repeat their terrible atrocities.

The issues of recidivism and the size of probation officer caseloads are intricately related. This is particularly evident in the area of research on effective and efficient caseload size. As previously indicated, little research has been done with regard to the most ideal caseload size. The research which has been done focuses on the effect of caseload size with respect to recidivism. The research methodology or model which has usually been used in an attempt to determine the effect of caseload size has focused on the extremes in caseload size. That is, either very large or very small caseloads. The former is designed to reflect the common caseload size while the latter reflects unique or unusual caseloads. Smaller caseloads are common in intensive probation supervision. In intensive probationary supervision the underlying assumption is that the smaller the caseload, the more effective the supervision and, consequently, the less recidivism. In fact, however, the data suggests that caseload size is not a significant predictor of reduced recidivism for either adults or juveniles. Specifically, simply reducing caseload size is not highly correlated with successful reduction of recidivism.[12] As is often the case with respect to human behavior, the limited research which has been done suggests that any reduction of recidivism is a result of multiple causes. In particular some combination of the following factors seem to have some positive effect in reducing recidivism: smaller caseloads, differential treatment of each offender in the community according to the individual's specialized correctional needs, an appropriate treatment setting and an appropriate matching of the offender's personality with that of the prospective probation officer.[12]

Predicated upon the views that probation may have become pointless,[11] ineffective as a means of social control,[3,] consistently confronted with insufficient funding, and an increasing need for additional probation officers,[11] it has been suggested that the role of probation officer should be strictly limited to that of a supervisor. There are, however, still other experts who favor the service provider role. Such programs must also resolve the critical issues of the complex range of offender needs and the broad range of human and social services available. In other words, those who proffer the model of the probation officer as a "supervisor only" posit that individuals cannot and do not need to be fully knowledgeable or professionally trained in all or even one of the various human service fields in order to be an effective and successful probation supervisor for offenders. As a matter of fact, the real challenge of probation is the ability to provide assistance, guidance and perhaps even friendship within the political structures of the criminal justice system and in spite of limited resources.[3] More recently, Cole noted that most probation officers who have training in the social service arena are most likely to adopt a rehabilitative or counseling perspective as opposed to supervision only.[4] In the Chapter about casemanagement with probationers and parolees on electronic monitoring which follows later in this book, the authors present a model for working with offenders which, hopefully, helps to resolve this supervisory-counselor issue.

THE ROLE OF THE PROBATION OFFICER

The issue of the role of the probation officer is a complex one. It is not simply a matter of the supervisor versus the service-provider. Nor is the debate strictly the result of recent events. The role definition and role expectation have been dynamic and fluid. Cole[3,4] traces its development through five historic phases and in doing so presents, by far, one of the best historical-analytical views of this phenomenon.

In the first phase, the probation officer took a holistic approach to his or her client. That is, they were concerned about and involved with the various aspects of the daily life of the offender. These aspects included the family, employment, social life, recreation, leisure, education and religious or moral life. In addition, it was anticipated that the officers would serve as positive role models and provide appropriate moral influence upon those they supervised. This can be designated as the casework model of probation.

In the second phase, therapeutic counseling was added to the role. Casework was not eliminated but much greater emphasis was given to therapeutic responses in the structure or confines of the probation supervisor's office as opposed to the daily settings in the life of the offender. This meant that counseling was confined to the office setting as a kind of structured therapeutic milieu. This was consistent with the development of psychology in the first quarter of the Twentieth Century, and particularly with the ideology of the Rankian School. This approach seemed to signal a change in that the probation officer could now be viewed as a monitor or supervisor appointed by the community to ensure that societal value systems were upheld. This change reflected new expectations that the officer would focus more on assisting offenders in resolution of specific emotional or social issues. This, of course, had significant parallels with clinical social work and clinical psychology models. Any such model, of course, permits considerable latitude on the part of the probation officer in analyzing the needs of each specific client and in designing the appropriate probation plan for the client. At the same time, this model assigned considerable responsibility to the individual officer with regard to accountability. Equally important was the fact that offenders were no longer considered passive observers in their own treatment. Rather, a part of the probation process included strategies for involving them in their own rehabilitation, reintegration or resocialization.

In the third phase, the offender was expected to take even more responsibility for the necessary social and behavioral changes necessary for his or her own successful reintegration into society. During the 1960's probation plans shifted from a focus on insight-development to a focus on very concrete problem resolution. This may be characterized as a reality-therapy approach. In particular, this included a variety of life coping skills such personal health, basic money management, schooling, interpersonal skills, communication, job interviewing, employment, housing, and utilization of appropriate community and agency services via referral. This effectively ended a model which fixed upon an office-based kind of psychotherapy. The role expectations of probation officers in this new role identify what can be labeled the advocate model. In this role the probation officer serves as an advocate or one who stands in front of or with the offender in his/her daily attempts to negotiate his or her life in both the public and private sectors. As the designation implies, the officer is an advocate for the offender with public and private service providers, rather than the actual vehicle for delivering these herself or himself.

New developments in the 1970's altered this latter model. In particular, an increasing concern emerged with respect to lowering the security risk to individuals and society embodied in the probated offender. Thus, rehabilitation and reintegration became secondary in importance to the dangers the offender was thought to provide and in reducing this threat. The model could perhaps be described as the community security monitor. Technical parole violations were more important than the fact that an offender might be making significant progress in becoming a useful and law abiding citizen. The policing-supervising- revoking officer was the ideal model.

Finally, the decade of the 1980's can be viewed as a time in which classification with respect to the needs, risks and potential rehabilitation of the offender were predominate. Perhaps this could be identified with the legal concept of the reasonably foreseen risk. In other words, the concern with reconciling the offender and the community is a part of the probation officer's role. However, this is balanced with a vigilant concern about risks with the realistic possibilities for the offender to live successfully in the community. In the 1990's, we seem to be continuing with the approach of the 1980's.

SUMMARY AND CONCLUSIONS

Probation is the remanding of an individual, as a result of criminal behaviors, to specified conditions of supervision within the community. This judgment permits the community to test the perception that this individual, in spite of his/her criminal behavior, can successfully avoid such behavior in the future. At the same time, it permits the offender to demonstrate or prove that this is, indeed, an accurate assessment of his or her situation. Probation is, thus, both a penalty within the justice system and a correctional practice within that system. In most instances, an individual who is placed on probation will not be incarcerated unless the conditions of probation are violated. This is a contrast with the practice of parole in which the individual is released to the community from a situation of incarceration.

There is some discussion among criminal justice professionals with respect to both who has the actual responsibility and authority over the probation system and who ought to have this responsibility and authority. On the one hand, arguments can be made that the practice is part of the judicial function and, as such, is commonly administered by the court system. On the other hand, it is a practice which occurs after the judicial process is completed and a penalty has been assessed by the court system. An important argument for administering it through the correctional system is that all of the other aspects of that system are then accessible to probation departments. It is contended that administration through the judiciary avoids the stigma for the offender that is a part of the correctional system. Additional arguments can be made for one system or the other.

Scholars in the field of criminal justice do not agree on the origins of probation. However, its development is commonly attributed to the efforts of John Augustus of Boston, Massachusetts. The date which is assigned to the development of probation in the United States is 1841. It is important to recognize the roots of probation in English Common Law. Concepts in Common Law such as benefit of clergy, judicial review and recognizance presage the practice of probation.

The earliest development of the practice of probation in the United States occurred as a result of the development of the juvenile court system. The establishment of the first juvenile court occurred in 1899. By 1925 all of the states were using probation for juveniles. However, it was not until 1956 that all of the states were using probation for adults. It is important to note that probation is the most frequently used form of punishment today in both juvenile and adult corrections.

The growth of probation has not been without criticism. Among the problems which critics note are caseload size and lack of supervision. Although research has not clarified what constitutes the ideal or most effective or efficient caseload, there is, without a doubt, a caseload size beyond which it is unrealistic to assume that a probation officer can even keep in contact with offenders, much less provide supervision or counseling. If some form of advocacy, therapy or life assistance is intended via probation, then the practical limits of time and interaction would require even smaller caseloads. A second criticism is that such programs are little more effective than incarceration. However, the telling element is that probation is less costly. Both of these criticisms also highlight the fact that there is limited data available by which to make judgments about the effectiveness of probation.

The controversy with respect to caseload size also underscores the various models of probation which have emerged in the practice of probation. The first model was that of the caseworker. Key to this approach is the holistic concern for and involvement with the probationer. This was the dominant model of probationary practice until the mid-1920's. Beginning the 1920's, the treatment model emerged as an addition to the practice model.   The significance of this shift lies in the fact that the role of the probation officer began to become more limited and specific. In particular, the probation officer was expected to focus upon therapeutic models and practices. By the 1960's the treatment model had become the dominant approach in the practice of probation. During the 1960's a third variant of the role of the probation officer developed. This was the role of the advocate. This role, as the designation suggests, anticipates the role of the probation officer as an advocate for the probationer. In some respects this represents a return to the holistic concept. It may, indeed, be nothing more than "old wine in new bottles". With this model, the probation officer was expected to primarily play out roles in the community on behalf of his or her probationer such as, a broker of community services and a locator of community resources. The 1970's produced an increasing concern about the dangers that probated offenders represented in society. Probation officers became community police, supervisors and probation revocation judges. Finally, in the 1980's this model once again included a concern for the possibility that offenders might change socially and behaviorally to the extent that they could be a full and functioning part of society. The concern for risk was still an important function of the probation officer role.   It was, however, balanced with a concern with returning or keeping the offender in his or her community. It also involved a genuine concern with attempting to assess the realistic possibility of the latter. More than a change in philosophies, the development of different models of probationary roles and services may reflect, instead, a practical political and economic response to the issues of increasing numbers of offenders assigned to probation and concomitant limited economic resources available to provide sufficient probation officers, services and programs.

These problems also led to several specific variations in the practice of probation itself which will be discussed in detail in the next Chapter: (1)

probation subsidies; (2) volunteers in probation; (3) pretrial services; (4) intensive probation; (5) shock probation; (6) restitution; (7) job banks; (8) complex offender programs; and, (9) community resource management teams. The process of probation also requires a familiarity with the conditions of probation, the process by which probation is revoked and the use of probation risk scales. These issues will also be discussed in the following Chapter.

An understanding of the definitions of probation, its historical development, the changes that have occurred in the system over time and the process of probation itself are all essential to any discussion or understanding of the viability of house arrest and electronic monitoring of parolees and probationers. That was the intention of this Chapter.

NOTES

1.   Lee H. Bowker. Corrections: The Science and the Art (New York: Macmillan Publishing Company, 1982).

2.   Calvin J. Larson. Crime-Justice and Society (Bayside, New York: General Hall, Inc., 1984).

3.   George F. Cole. The American System of Criminal Justice (Monterey, CA: Brooks/Cole Publishing Co., 1983).

4.   George F. Cole. The American System of Criminal Justice (6th ed.) (Pacific Grove, CA: Brooks/ Cole Publishing Co., 1992).

5.   Stan Stojkovic and Rick Lovell. Corrections, an Introduction (Cincinnati, OH: Anderson Publishing Co., l992).

6.   Sue Titus Reid. The Correctional System: An Introduction (New York: Holt, Rinehart and Winston, 1981).

7.   Belinda Rodgers McCarthy and Bernard J. McCarthy, Jr. Community Based Corrections (Pacific Grove, CA: Brooks/Cole Publishing Co., 1991).

8.   Henry W. Mannle and J. David Hirschel. Fundamentals of Criminology (Englewood Cliffs, NJ: Prentice Hall, Inc., 1988).

9.   Peter C. Kratcoski and Lucille D. Kratcoski. Juvenile Delinquency (Englewood Cliffs, NJ: Prentice-Hall, Inc., 1979).

10.   Todd R. Clear and George F. Cole. American Corrections. (2nd ed.) (Pacific Grove, CA: Brooks/Cole Publishing Co., 1990).

11.   Stephen Gettinger. Intensive Supervision: Can It Rehabilitate Probation? in John J. Sullivan and Joseph L. Victor (eds.) Annual Editions: Criminal Justice (Guilford, CT: Dushkin Publishing Group, Inc., 1985).

12.   Gerald D. Robin. Introduction to the Criminal Justice System (3rd ed.) (New York: Harper and Row Publishers, 1987).

CHAPTER 2

RECENT DEVELOPMENTS IN PROBATION

INTRODUCTION
There are several recent developments in the institution of probation which
need consideration prior to any discussion of house arrest or electronic
monitoring. These include (1) probation subsidy; (2) volunteers in probation;
(3) pretrial services and pretrial diversion; (4) intensive probation; (5) shock
probation and split sentencing; (6) restitution; (7) job banks; (8) complex
offender programs; and (9) community resource management teams. These
innovations or changes in probation can be viewed as responses to the
problems, crises and need for changes referred to in Chapter One. In
particular, they represent responses to the overloading of the probation system
by the assignment of ever increasing numbers of offenders to the system and
the attendant personnel, economic and administrative problems which
followed as a result. The question remains as to whether these innovations
make probation a more humane remedy than incarceration. In the view of the
authors, these innovations do make the process more humane while forcing
greater levels of responsibility on probationers.

PROBATION SUBSIDY

Probation subsidy represents a process of providing financial incentives to
discourage counties from incarcerating offenders and to encourage these
governmental entities to maintain offenders on probation. Ordinarily this
approach includes supplemental funding which permits or requires reduced of
caseload size to insure that serious offenders could be given special time and
attention. The supplemental funding which is acquired by the probation
departments can be used to provide a vast array of supervision alternatives.
These subsidies have been used to create a special group of probation
supervisors, fund innovative training for them and provide new equipment or
technology where appropriate. They were intended to result in reduced case
load sizes.[1] Although this innovation increased the prestige of special
supervision officers, unfortunately, it also created dissatisfaction among
probation personnel who were assigned to traditional caseloads. Whether this
approach did, in fact, increase the effectiveness of probation officers has
remained an unanswered question. A review by Cole of research in this area
indicates that such subsidies did not significantly influence incarceration rates

with respect to comparisons between recipient and non recipient counties.[1] In other words, several of the researchers posited that the subsidy had little effect in lowering incarceration rates. It was hypothesized that regardless of the subsidies, incarceration rates had begun to decrease toward the end of the 1960's. This program elicited considerable opposition from police chiefs and county sheriffs. It is now on the decline in most states.

VOLUNTEERS IN PROBATION

Volunteers in probation characterizes one essential component of probation as John Augustus originally conceived it. That is, probation officers were perceived as having an obligation "to befriend." This program was initiated in Michigan in 1959 by Judge Keith J. Leinhouts.[1] It involved pairing a citizen volunteer with a specific probationer. The volunteer would be a mentor or role model in much the same way as the Big Brothers and Big Sisters Programs operate with children and adolescents. Each volunteer was under the direct supervision of a specific probation officer. This venture ultimately culminated in the creation of a national organization of probation volunteers and volunteers in other aspects of corrections and prevention.[2] In effect, the volunteers supplemented the expertise of the probation officer by assuming tasks that would require more of his or her time, thus, providing more opportunity for that officer to work with the most critical needs of the client. Furthermore, these individuals served as positive role models, as friends and as someone who could assist the offenders in understanding the criminal justice system and its requirements as well as understanding social norms and learning how to reintegrate into society. Although this program has been extensively implemented nationwide, as with so many of the variations in probation, it has received considerable criticism. In this instance, the criticism came most often from probation officers concerned about their own employment, roles and professionalism.[1] The concern which is common to professionals in the criminal justice system with respect to nonprofessionals is that offenders are very successful at manipulating them to their own ends and not necessarily their own ultimate good. This concern has been expressed regarding this type of program.

PRETRIAL SERVICES AND PRETRIAL DIVERSION

Pretrial services is a concept which refers to a broad range of possibilities involving pretrial release services and the diversion of individuals who are diverted from various aspects of the criminal justice system.[1] This innovation in probation is manifested in formal organizational structures created specifically for these purposes within probation departments.[2] The main focus of these programs is upon first time offenders and offenders with less serious criminal histories. Pretrial services and pretrial diversion permits such individuals to be released into the community on their own recognizance in the event that they cannot make bail. It has been a common practice in many probation departments for probation officers to provide background information which is essential to the judge in making a decision with respect to whether to release these suspects. In the formal pretrial organizations outlined here, probation officers are assigned the same task.

In some of these programs, services such as counseling are provided prior to any adjudication or other disposition of the case. These services are designed to focus upon effective and efficient mechanisms for resolving any problems that the alleged offender may be experiencing. Then, regardless of the outcome of the decision of the judge, the individual has already been equipped for a higher probability of success upon his or her return to the community. In certain situations, offenders using these services have often had the charges against them dropped and their records cleared.

Pretrial diversion, although often confused with pretrial services, is a different, although related, idea. The use of pretrial diversion increased significantly during the 1980's. Many programs were developed to divert the offender from the criminal justice process entirely. This included programs such as drug and alcohol rehabilitation. Probationary conditions are still imposed upon the offender. But, if the offender fulfills these conditions, and is successful in the diversion program, then the offender's criminal record may be eliminated.[3]

INTENSIVE PROBATION SUPERVISION

Intensive probation supervision, as the label implies, involves a more intensive application of the traditional concept and practices of probation supervision. It has been argued that the perceived shortcomings or criticisms of traditional probation, as outlined earlier, have culminated in this more intensive version of the traditional probation program. Intensive probation supervision is characterized by more frequent contacts with the probationer by the officer, more rigorous supervision and by attempts to convince the client that even though the supervision is not moment-to-moment, it is an extensive and thorough monitoring. Further, the structure and expectations are predicated upon the idea that sanctions will, indeed, be forthcoming, if the conditions of probation are violated. This is the message that is clearly communicated to the probationer.

These types of programs are designed to respond to and reduce or eliminate the perceived causes of the criminal behavior and to provide appropriate deterrence from such behavior in the future. There is some evidence to suggest that these programs do work and are less expensive than incarceration.[4] However, both Champion,[3] and McCarthy and McCarthy,[2] underscore the mixed reactions on the part of the public to the programs and the conflicting data on the results. Like so many of the community corrections approaches or alternative models, the results with respect to success or failure are seriously skewed as a result of the client selection process and the nature of the offenders assigned to these programs.

SHOCK PROBATION

Shock probation is a unique innovation on the concept of probation in that it combines incarceration with probation. Usually, the offender is remanded to a correctional facility or bootcamp for a traditional sentence. They must then "earn" their freedom through good behavior and cooperation with counselors. As the first part of the term implies, the intent is to shock the offender with respect to the seriousness of his/her behavior and to bring into awareness the extreme consequences which have resulted from the behavior. That is, the offense that was committed has led to a loss of freedom and rights and has resulted in incarceration under less than ideal circumstances. It is anticipated that selected offenders, given a "taste" or a brief experience of those consequences will, if permitted, leave incarceration to embark upon a law abiding life. The key to the effective use of this procedure is for the actual incarceration to be brief and that the fact that an early release is unanticipated or earned.[5] It is intended for use with first and second time offenders. This split sentence concept is a means of utilizing both a community corrections approach and an incarceration approach. It is thought that such a short period of incarceration will not have attendant upon it all of the negative aspects of a full incarceration.[4]

This innovation has not been without its critics. One research study suggested that recidivism rates for offenders who had received shock probation were not significantly different from those who had not been subjected to shock incarceration.[5] And, some of its critics contend that data from the behavioral sciences indicates that rewards and reinforcements are far more important in generating and sustaining behavioral changes than are punishments. Further, the National Advisory Commission on Criminal Justice Standards and Goals raises additional objections, citing data from sociological labeling theory that suggests that incarceration leads to stigmatization. This phenomenon is one component of what has been described as a process that "...defeats the purpose of probation, which is the earliest possible reintegration of the offender into the community." (P. 335).[5] It is hypothesized that in addition to stigmatization, the brief period of incarceration exposes the individual "...to the destructive effects of institutionalization...[and] disrupts his life in the community....". (P. 335).[5]

RESTITUTION

Restitution is one of the newer innovations in probation. It has gained considerable support in a short period of time. In this practice, probation and the successful fulfillment of the sentence requires some compensation of the crime victim by the offender. This may involve specific financial compensation (financial restitution) to the victim or some other appropriate compensation, or it may involve a compensation to the community by donation of time or other service by the offender (service restitution).[4] This form of restitution is, in one respect, a modification of the intent of "retributive justice" promulgated in criminal law. That is, "A criminal court ...[does not] award damages to a victim".(P. 9).[6] Rather, a "violation of criminal law...constitutes an offense against the state." (P. 9).[6] Thus, the justice system is assumed to be rational and there is no element of personal or individual revenge in the punishment. Service restitution is a modification of this notion in that no restitution is made to the victim, but is provided to the society. Although this does implement the principle of restitution, it continues to "...ignore the fate of the victim." (P. 338).[7] Fines and even service restitution reflect "...a payment 'in kind' to society". (P. 338).[7] Such "community service" is especially appropriate for offenses in which there is no readily identifiable victim.

Financial restitution, on the other hand, is a radical modification of the concept of retributive justice. That is, damages or compensation are awarded directly to the victim. This approach is designed to financially compensate a victim for his or her loss. The underlying goal or assumption of this innovation is that the justice system and the offender should not ignore the impact of the crime on the victim. Further, it is presumed that the offender is more likely to internalize accountability for the behavior if some cost is attached to it. As already indicated, the nature of the cost may vary. It is important to recognize that probation is commonly used in crimes against property and against businesses. In this context, the penalty may be more meaningful both to the offender and to the victim than is incarceration or traditional probation.[4]

There are, of course, situations in which there is absolutely no way that the offender could ever be able to compensate the victim. This may be true because the skills or abilities of the offender would never enable that individual to generate even a modest income and, thus, repay the victim while supporting himself or herself. It can also be illustrated by situations when the offense is of such great financial magnitude that the offender, even with highly marketable skills, would never be able to accumulate the necessary funds to repay the loss to the victim. Finally, there are other losses, such as the death or injury of a family member who is the main source of income or provides other essential family service, which can never be compensated for in any financial sense but can be matched or minimally replaced with respect to selected functions. In such cases, symbolic financial restitution and service restitution to the victim and society can be combined. This represents a kind of psychological compensation.

Service restitution can be almost any service of benefit to the community or the victim. An important aspect of this type of restitution is the attempt to make it meaningful and related to the nature of the offense. It should be noted that service restitution is a term generally reserved for services performed for the benefit of the community or society. However, some judges have required behaviors on the part of offenders which can be designated as both service restitution and financial restitution to the victim. Further, it should be understood that all payments to the state represent symbolic restitution to the state. With respect to the victim, both financial restitution and service restitution come closer to exacting justice and possible "revenge" than do ordinary justice system penalties.

It is essential to differentiate the concept of restitution from victim compensation. In service restitution and financial restitution programs, offenders actually reside at restitution centers. Compensation, on the other hand, can be exacted even without the imposition of the restitution center. In the same sense, restitution is frequently imposed as a part of probation without requiring residence at a special facility. Many variations of this concept have emerged throughout the country. Such programs are the outcome of specific legislation and innovative responses by judges.

JOB BANKS

Job banks represent probationary approaches in which unique or special efforts are made to assist offenders in improving their job skills and employment prospects. Such programs generally emphasize "coping skills" training relevant to obtaining and sustaining employment. In some cases education and job training or retraining are essential aspects of the programs. Bowker cites research which suggests positive results from such an approach.

In a comparison of probationer participants and nonparticipants in these kinds of programs it was discovered that the most significant variable that correlated with success in the program was having a job. However, he also notes that critics have argued that the most significant variable was simply participation in the program.[5] Furthermore, it is important to emphasize that probation programs have stressed and attempted to include a focus upon job skills for a considerable number of years. The ideology underlying this approach in traditional probationary programs was the thought that employment reduces recidivism and programs which foster employment also further the goal of reducing repeat offenses. Historically, the idea of "work" has permeated all Western-culture social welfare systems. Unemployment is a major problem for many offenders but some feel that it is unfair to provide services to offenders that are not available to the law-abiding.

COMPLEX OFFENDER PROJECTS

Complex offender projects envision the role of the probation officer as a counselor or therapist. Because of this, specially trained personnel are needed to implement these programs. Specifically, persons with appropriate training in psychology, social work, psychiatric nursing, or vocational rehabilitation counseling are required. Several additional personnel with less specific skills and training, e.g., mental health paraprofessionals, are also essential for assisting in these programs. This type of program could be said to harken back to the therapeutic emphasis of probation programs that existed from the 1920's through the early 1960's. However, the programs also have elements of what has been called the "advocate model". These approaches were discussed in Chapter One. In addition, this approach requires that the offender be placed upon intensive probation supervision.

The particular "spin" of complex offender projects is that these programs allow offenders to negotiate with their probation officers or with other correctional personnel regarding certain aspects of the treatment approach and/or the probation plan. It is a method for involving the offender in his or her treatment. In this manner, it makes the offender assume some responsibility for the outcomes of the treatment and the probation plan. To be successful, complex offender projects require probationary staff members who are knowledgeable about mental health approaches, well-trained and very professional.

The similarity between complex offender projects and intensive probation supervision is suggested by the fact that contacts with individual clients are fairly frequent throughout the week and also are supplemented with numerous telephone contacts. Contact hours with various staff members may be as high as 20 hours a week in the event of a crisis.[5] Of course, the intent of a program of this sort is to increase the ability of the individual to adapt to the local community and the larger society and to be able to function successfully in both of these environments. In addition, it introjects the medical (psychotherapeutic) model into the probation program. Some research indicates that when these kinds of programs are compared with traditional programs, the therapeutic gains are modest and the costs are high.[5] However, this is a criticism that is commonly made about all types of programs that have a psychotherapeutic focus. The officer's power and duty to revoke liberty confounds attempts to act as principal therapist to the client.

COMMUNITY RESOURCE MANAGEMENT TEAMS

Community resource management teams promote the idea of providing the offender with direct assistance with problem solving while role modeling appropriate behaviors. This is in contrast to traditional probationary practices which focus mainly upon one-to-one counseling in office settings. Here, the idea is to use a team of resource persons as service providers on behalf of the offender. The role of the probation officer in this model is akin to that of a casemanager of a team of resource persons. In other words, the probation officer does not attempt to meet all of the needs of the probationer, but instead, he/she plays a significant role in marshalling and managing the resources needed to resolve the problems and crises experienced by the offender. Such programs may result in shared caseloads by officers and in sharing and marshalling the expertise of their fellow officers in solving particular client needs. In addition to the resources of each individual team member, in order to accomplish its goals the team may involve all available community resources, public and private.[4]

THE PROCESS OF PROBATION

There are three aspects of the process or actual operation of probation which remain for discussion. These are: (1) the conditions of probation; (2) the revocation of probation; and, (3) the use of probation risk scales. Of course, consideration of each of these reflects the historical development of probation and recent developments in this field. An understanding of these three aspects are critical to any discussion of house arrest and/or electronic monitoring.

Conditions of Probation

According to Robin, the limits on probation conditions are almost nonexistent.[4] Another way of expressing this is that an exceedingly diverse array of conditions of probation are common and tolerated in each community in this country. These conditions can include home detention and/or electronic monitoring. In fact, relatively limited guidance is provided by law with respect to imposing probation. That is, much is left to the discretion of the court.

The specific conditions of probation emerge from two sources. First, such conditions can be imposed from the rules that govern the probation department to which the offender is assigned. Such rules apply to all probationers. Second, the court can impose conditions at its own discretion and can be as innovative as it determines appropriate regarding any specific client. Their de facto nature is further evidenced by the practical reality that the only challenge to such conditions must be predicated upon the argument that they are not reasonable, have no relevance to the specific sentencing objectives or that they do not violate the constitutional rights of the probationer.[4]

Revocation of Probation

Probation can be considered to have two general outcomes. In the first situation, an offender can be deemed to have successfully fulfilled the conditions imposed by probation. In the second instance, the offender is judged to have committed an offense of such a serious nature while on probation that his or her probation must be revoked and he or she must be remanded to an institution. Or, some other element of the original punishment order must be imposed. Serious violations of this type may be generalized as: (1) arrest for a new crime; (2) failure to notify the court of changes in residence; and, (3) violation of conditions imposed by the court. The designation of violations of probation as "serious" implies that some behaviors may, in fact, violate the conditions of probation, but may be considered non-serious. In other words, it is essential to recognize that the probation officer, as in so much of the criminal justice process, has considerable latitude or discretion with regard to reporting a violation.[4]

Once the report is made, a process has been initiated which can lead to revocation and incarceration. It needs to be underscored that although the probation officer reports the violation, it is not the probation officer but the court that revokes probation. That is, it is the court which actually has the authority to ultimately revoke probation. At the same time, the offender "...is entitled to a dual revocation hearing that incorporates specified due process protection." (P. 443).[4] The initial hearing is designed to ascertain probable cause for revocation and determine if a fuller hearing is necessary. In the event of probable cause, a second hearing will be set. It is at the second hearing that an actual determination would be made to revoke probation. Constitutional safeguards are required at both stages.[4]

It is helpful to contrast revocation of probation with revocation of parole. In the former, the "...hearing is a judicial process, while the...[latter] is an administrative process." (P. 337).[5] Even if a probation officer exercises his or her discretion (option) to report a violation, revocation is not automatic. In fact, three possible outcomes can emanate from a revocation hearing: (1) no violation occurred; (2) a violation occurred but a reprimand is sufficient punishment; and, (3) a violation occurred and the offender is to be imprisoned or punished.[5]

Probation Risk Scales

From the very earliest uses of probation, attempts were made to determine which offenders would be most appropriate to be released back into society for an opportunity to prove that he or she was capable of remaining in the community, in spite of the fact that he or she had committed a crime. Many of the earliest measures reflected informal and subjective efforts. Quite frequently they incorporated the prejudices of the individuals empowered to make the decisions. Eventually the process became "scientific" as criminologists and professionals and practitioners developed and devised scales based upon empirical research techniques and statistical methods. Probation scales are presumed to be diagnostic as well as classification devices which are thought to have predictive power concerning the potential success of any given group of probationers. The baseline or normative points of the scales are derived from the performance of prior groups (cohorts) of probationers. In addition, these scales have utility for probation departments with respect to screening clients for the highest probability of success given the least amount of restrictive supervision. By assigning values to the variables on the scales related to a variety of characteristics of offenders that have been statistically determined to be significant, and by ranking each offender with respect to these values, an individual risk score can be derived.

Risk scales, like other sorts of psychosocial-diagnostic tests, are problematic. Champion concludes that they are inconsistent and are apt to vary, creating problems of consistency.[3] Bowker cites two specific problems. First, the inability to generalize from one population of offenders to another with respect to geographic location; second, the lack of reliability and validity between groups of offenders at different points in time. The latter suggests the significance of social conditions and historical circumstances in determining outcomes.[5]   However, juxtaposed to these potential weaknesses is the research which has been conducted on county and state probation risk scales in the United States. Bowker, for example, cites research conducted on eight of these scales.   The research indicated that in each case the scales did differentiate between success and failures of probationers. These studies also supported the idea of generalizability across various areas of the country.[5] In any case, it is important to note that these scales have a statistically higher level of predictive power or success than do judges or probation officers who often must make judicial decisions without the benefit of these scales. And, equally important is the finding that combining the clinical evaluations of the probation personnel with statistical prediction scales provides a higher degree of reliability in predicting success or failure of probationers than either method alone.[5]

Probation risk scales have been in use for a considerable period of time. Research and improved statistical techniques and computer capabilities facilitate continued refinement and increased predictive powers for the scales. Most probation departments have adopted various types of probation risk scales and have incorporated them into the assessments made at the local level by judges and probation officers.

COMMUNITY CORRECTIONS

Community corrections can probably be best and most simply understood as a point of view which embodies the idea that community-based programs and services, particularly those that are innovative in nature, are better responses to the issue of "dealing" with offenders than incarceration.   However, when we consider the term community corrections we must remember that some of these programs and services may only be "old wine in new bottles" while others may be "real" innovations. The most prudent course is to consider that history shows that most social welfare service responses to human problems are "not new under the sun".

The most powerful iteration of the idea of community corrections came about following the dissemination of a 1967 report by the President's Commission on Law Enforcement and Administration of Justice which championed the idea. Following this report, there was increased movement in the field of probation toward an approach to corrections which subsequently became labeled: "community corrections". The resurgence of community corrections after 1967 represents one of the most important developments in the field.

The most recent version of community corrections is a very interesting development because it represents both a philosophy of corrections and also describes and delineates a variety of separate, diverse, past, current or innovative correctional approaches under that label. Because of this feature, there is no common agreement in the field about what community corrections means. There is some general agreement, nevertheless, with the idea that community corrections today represents a smorgasbord of alternatives to incarceration which take three forms or have three purposes: (1) alternatives that are designed to be substitutes for prison sentences; (2) non-custodial penal measures; and, (3) measures which reduce the length of incarceration by offering an alternative which results in early release.[8]

SUMMARY AND CONCLUSIONS

Recent innovations in the field of probation include several specific variations in the practice of probation. In particular these include: (1) probation subsidies; (2) volunteers in probation; (3) pretrial services and pretrial diversion; (4) intensive probation; (5) shock probation and split sentences; (6) restitution; (7) job banks; (8) complex offender programs; (9) and, community resource management teams. Probation subsidies represent a process of providing financial incentives to discourage counties from incarcerating offenders and to encourage these governmental entities to maintain offenders on probation. Volunteers in probation involve citizens in the process of working with offenders. Pretrial services represent practices designed to assist the accused before he or she has even come to trial and/or been adjudicated guilty. Intensive probation is a more intense process of supervision than regular supervision. Shock probation represents an attempt to deter the offender through a brief incarceration, but to avoid the stigma and effects of long-term incarceration. Restitution denotes service provided to or financial replacement, by offenders, to victimized individuals or communities. Job banks represent a view that the key factor in preventing recidivism is employment and, thus, the focus of this program is on enabling offenders to gain and maintain employment. Complex offender projects provide intensive supervision and a probation team to provide assistance and therapy to the offender. Community resource management teams reflect the advocacy model in which the probation officer serves as a program resource locator and broker. Community corrections include a vast array of programs and services directed at offenders in order to provide them with community based alternatives to incarceration.

The process of probation requires a familiarity with the conditions of probation, the process by which probation is revoked and the use of probation risk scales. The conditions of probation describe the expectations which are imposed on the offender's behavior. Revocation can be an outcome of the violation of the conditions of probation. The probation officer has some discretion in determining whether a violation of the conditions of probation is serious enough to warrant revocation. The probation officer, however, does not have the authority to revoke probation. Revocation requires two hearings and constitutional safeguards. If probation is revoked, the original punishment and/or incarceration is imposed. Probation risk scales are instruments which measure the characteristics of an offender on statistically significant variables and when summed, provide a score predicting the probability that probation would have to be revoked for a specific offender.

The definition of probation, the historical development of probation, the changes which have occurred and the process of probation are all essential to any discussion of the viability of house arrest.   Now and in the future, attention will need to be directed at who will control probation programs, the nature of training for probation personnel, the goals of probation, the roles of   probation officers, the impact of caseload sizes, the relationship of traditional probationary approaches to innovations as well as the nature of the relationships among various innovations, and the issue of determining the most appropriate types of offenders for various programs within probation. In the Chapters which follow, these issues will be discussed again in relation to the use of electronic monitoring of probationers and parolees on house arrest.

NOTES

1.   George F. Cole. The American System of Criminal Justice (Monterey, CA: Brooks/Cole Publishing Co., 1983).

2.   Belinda Rodgers McCarthy and Bernard J. McCarthy, Jr. Community Based Corrections (Pacific Grove, CA: Brooks/Cole Publishing Co., 1991).

3.   Dean J. Champion. Probation and Parole in the United States (Columbus, OH: Merrill Publishing Co., 1990).

4.   Gerald D. Robin. Introduction to the Criminal Justice   System. (3rd ed.). (New York: Harper and Row, 1987).

5.   Lee H. Bowker. Corrections: The Science and the Art (New York: Macmillan Publishing Company, Inc., 1982).

6.   Martin R. Haskell and Lewis Yablonsky. Crime and Delinquency (3rd ed.) (New York: Rand McNally College   Publishing Company, 1978).

7.   Abraham S. Blumberg. Criminal Justice: Issues and Ironies (2nd. ed.) (New York: New Viewpoints, 1979).

8.   Antony A. Vas. Alternatives to Prison: Punishment, Custody and the Community (Newbury Park, CA: Sage Publications, 1990).

CHAPTER 3

THEORETICAL BASIS FOR ELECTRONIC MONITORING

INTRODUCTION

Almost since imprisonment's inception as the principal method of punishing criminal offenders, its efficacy in reducing crime has been questioned. Historically, efforts at punishment of the offender have sprung from at least four ideological positions (or combinations thereof):

1. The perspective that punishment must also contain a rehabilitative component. This idea has existed since at least the Eighteenth Century in Western criminology. The point is made that punishment ought to be used reluctantly and that education (usually in the form of moral uplifting) is the preferred treatment strategy. Over time, the key point inherent in this approach has been the idea of the usefulness of social and psychological knowledge in corrections. With this point of view, correctional approaches toward rehabilitation focus on the choices made by offenders.

2. The notion that prison should be used to confine offenders so that they will be unable to bring harm or discomfort to others. This is the idea of punishment as incapacitation, at least for a time, or permanently, as in the case of capital punishment. Historically, this is probably the oldest notion about how to deal with the criminal offender.

3. The view that offenders will know that they will face personal jeopardy and punishment if they bring harm to others. This is the idea of individual deterrence from crime. It is believed that the notion of swift and sure individual punishment for each and every instance of crime will help deter criminal behavior.

4. The point-of-view that punishment ought to make a distinct impression upon offenders and, in so doing, deter others from crime. This is the idea of general deterrence. It is thought that deterrence will occur if prospective criminals view punishment for criminal acts as severe and certain. This is particularly true if such acts are well publicized or if individual criminals are stigmatized or draw notoriety for their crimes. Examples of this are often played out in the media, particularly during public punishment phases such as the execution of a murderer.

However, despite many attempts at reformation of penal institutions, and the playing-out, at one time or another, of one or more of these ideologies, the most noteworthy innovations in correctional policies and practices during the last century have been in the area of community-based alternatives to incarceration. Therefore, the purpose of this chapter is to explore the theoretical basis for electronic monitoring which is principally based upon various notions about criminal diversion and community-based alternatives to incarceration.

Apprehension over the criminogenic effects of imprisonment and the need to reduce correctional budgets are the motivating factors behind these attempts at community-based alternatives to incarceration. In addition, it seems clear that each series of reforms in community corrections has reflected the political tone of its era, and program goals have thus alternated between rehabilitation and various types of punishment orientations.

In this Chapter, the principal components of the community correction programs that emerged from the "rehabilitative ideal" of the past are juxtaposed against the current generation of programs emerging from a "control oriented" punishment perspective as alternatives to incarceration. While the goals and philosophies of rehabilitation and control/punishment oriented program strategies for coping with offenders are very different, their structures and effects on the offender are similar.

IDEOLOGICAL BASES OF COMMUNITY CORRECTION PROGRAMS

Within the last two decades, a number of theorists in criminology have addressed the issue of community corrections.
Ball and Lilly, for example, proposed that a dialectical criminology that would consider the way in which perceptions of appropriate punishment change over time was needed. According to Ball and Lilly's theoretical perspective, new alternative sentencing policies stand little likelihood of adoption unless they are communicable and understandable in terms of the conceptions of social reality dominant in any particular era. This cogent perspective also asserts that such programs must be compatible with the prevalent ethos of the era in which they are to be employed.[1] In practical terms this means that to be successfully adopted, alternative sentences must be sufficiently harsh to meet public demands for deterrence, retribution and incapacitation but flexible enough to be cost-effective. This last criterion implies that they must have a demonstrable effect on recidivism. Therefore, they also must succeed in altering certain aspects of offenders' behavior.

By providing tentative general statements of the basic methods of these new and old programs a theoretical comparison can be made between them. A comparison of this type shows that many commonalities do exist between the methods used to rehabilitate offenders and those used to deter and incapacitate them in the community. That is, despite the great variability in their socio-political justification and basic goals, community-correction sentences that stress rehabilitation have much in common with those emphasizing control and punishment.

Much of the literature on corrections appears to assume that deterrence and incapacitation are, at least to some extent, antithetical to reformation. This assumption usually results from over generalizations of research on the impact of total institutions. Review of recidivism rates and similar data on intermediate sentencing programs suggest that such a supposition is not fully justified.[2]

According to Zedlewski, deterrence and incapacitation are requisite elements if community corrections is to have a deterrent effect competitive with that of incarceration.[3] That is, community corrections must be as effective as incarceration in reducing the number of people willing to commit crimes. Two important concepts are at issue here: "Deterrence effectiveness" and "incapacitation effectiveness". Deterrence effectiveness depends on how would-be offenders react to increased risks (i.e., whether potential new offenders will avoid crime under such conditions). Whereas, incapacitation effectiveness depends on the identification of the most frequent offenders and on the losses incurred by concentrating on frequent offenders. Existing data tentatively endorse the case for more incapacitation.[3]

Other writers have alleged that the dominance of the rehabilitative ideal in past decades crippled the deterrence effects sought by judges, legislators and the public.[4] While this may or may not have been true of past innovations in sentencing, the converse is patently false-the goals of rehabilitation may be better served by cost-cutting programs that seek primarily to deter and control than by earlier, more humanistic approaches. The assertion is that the structured lifestyle imposed on offenders by alternative sentencing programs, though formulated to ease control, effectively serves the latent function of rehabilitation.

An analysis of the basic similarities that exist between the rehabilitative correctional programs of the 1965-75 period and the control oriented alternative programs that have emerged in the last decade is useful for several reasons. First, discussion of the manifest and latent functions of community based correctional programs are essential to an understanding of program design and planning. Secondly, such discussion allows for an understanding of the internal conflict experienced by probation/parole officers and other criminal justice system functionaries working in these programs brought on by their alternating between change and control agent roles. Currently, probation officers directed to be less concerned with the provision of services, such as counseling, employment assistance, and more concerned with such things as drug testing, curfew violations, employment verifications, arrest checks, surveillance, and revocation procedures is an example of this type of role conflict.[5] Thirdly, an explicit theoretical statement of the utility of community-based sentences helps in understanding empirical evaluations of the rehabilitative and deterrent effects of both types of programs, as well as their selection methods. And, finally, such a discussion is necessary to an understanding to the expansion of control oriented alternative sentencing programs to include more serious categories of offenders. According to Petersilia, such expansion is necessary if these recent innovations in community corrections are to be truly useful in relieving correctional budgets and institutional crowding.[2]

THE SOCIO-POLITICAL CONTEXT OF ALTERNATIVE SENTENCING

The introduction and improvement of indeterminate sentences, offender classification systems, and a plethora of training and counseling programs typified early attempts to improve the correctional system. Theoretical efficacy in rehabilitating criminal offenders largely justified these measures. Similar justifications justified the later changes in U.S. correctional policies focused on community based treatment programs. The widespread acceptance of labeling theory and its implications in the 1965-75 period fueled attempts to divert offenders from the criminal justice system entirely. Many see this phase of correctional development as the zenith of the rehabilitative ideal. Although well-intentioned, this series of programs didn't provide cost-effective remedies to crime and recidivism.[6] With the political conservatism of the mid-1970's, control theory became the dominant approach to crime and corrections. From this philosophy emerged a group of sentencing alternatives that are different from their predecessors in their philosophies and goals. If only to a limited degree, this shift shows a more general rejection of the liberal rehabilitation ethos of earlier decades.

Still, rejection of the rehabilitative ideal is far from complete. According to public opinion polls, it appears that the public still acknowledges the need for rehabilitation and community corrections but seeks greater control over offenders than traditional probation and parole officers have generally exercised.[7]

Due to the arrival of neo-conservative sentiments among the public beginning in the early 1980's, and the resulting emphasis on budget cutting and social control, the system's goals have turned from rehabilitation to retribution, deterrence, and incapacitation. In fact, because of public sentiment, these goals have come with a vengeance. One result has been prison overcrowding. Furthermore, the combination of conservative politics and prison overcrowding led to renewed interest in alternative sentences guided by a philosophy more attuned to punishment than rehabilitation.[7] Illustrating the problems facing the community correctional system are the facts that in 1985, 1.65% of males in U.S. were under some form of correctional supervision, representing an increase of 600,000 offenders since 1983. By 1985, 64.4% of the 2,904,979 adult offenders under correctional supervision were on probation. Because of overcrowding in prisons and jails, almost every state has alternate methods of intensive community-based programs.[6]

Designed to reduce jail/prison populations and improve the management of traditional probation caseloads, the new alternative sentencing programs are premised and evaluated on criteria that reflect cost-effective deterrence or incapacitation. In addition, these alternative sentencing programs have focused on the benefits accruing to the offender and the community by avoiding incarceration.[8] Typical of these innovations are shock probation, intensively supervised probation (ISP), house arrest and electronic monitoring, restitution, and community service.[2] Victim-offender mediation and lawsuits for punitive damages can supplement these programs. Such sanctions are usually designed for implementation by existing agencies, often without the addition of new staff positions. Counseling and other measures aimed at reforming the offender are strictly of secondary concern in the design of those programs that stress the surveillance and control of offenders. This often results in role-conflict for probation officers, who are trained in and oriented to rehabilitation, rather than social control.[2] Simultaneously, the long-term cost-effectiveness of sentences becomes very dubious if it is assumed that incapacitation, rather than behavior change, results from intermediate sentencing.

These alternatives to incarceration have been encouraged by scholars who have recognized the inherent contradictions between rehabilitation and imprisonment, as well as by the public, which has increasingly come to define traditional community correctional programs as a mere "slap on the wrist" for offenders. To assure public safety, as well as to satisfy the demands of judges, legislators, and the voting public, intermediate sanctioning programs have tended to stress the punitive, deterrent and incapacitating potentials of community corrections over that of rehabilitation.

Because it lacks a singular motivating principle like the rehabilitative ideal, the new generation of alternative sentences is more diverse in the formats it employs than were earlier models of the correctional process. Also contributing to this diversity are the goals of various programs. Some seek to improve case management, while others are aimed at reducing jail or prison populations. As goals vary, so also do selection criteria; staff attitudes toward, and expectations of clients; methods of control and reform; and evaluation standards.

THE REHABILITATION MODEL

Most of the innovations in twentieth century correctional practices have been based on the rehabilitative ideal and stressed counseling, "insight," vocational development and pre-trial diversion. The therapeutic community is, in many ways, the epitome of these efforts toward a rehabilitation-oriented correctional system. These facilities combine a broad range of rehabilitative techniques with a high degree of social structure and solidarity.[9] Therapeutic communities can, of course, be considered a form of intermediate sentence in themselves. While by definition they are residential facilities for persons with behavioral problems, they lack the extremes of bureaucratization, custodial security, and coercion that typify the total institution. Therapeutic communities accepting probated clients certainly involve an element of coercion, but no physical methods are employed to prevent escapes.[9] Thus, they cannot offer the punitive and incapacitating impact sought by current innovations. For these reasons, along with the solidarity and quasi-democratic procedures that typify most therapeutic communities, this form of rehabilitation program is seen as the epitome of humanistic attempts to correct offender behavior. Therapeutic communities are, more precisely, rehabilitative milieux.

Fundamentally, the therapeutic community represents a rehabilitative milieu in which a large number of more or less scientifically validated psychosocial behavior change strategies are employed jointly on a single population. The focus is commonly on individual or group therapy approaches. Prior research has shown that therapeutic communities can be extremely effective in eliciting permanent behavior change in a variety of populations.[10]   But, they are plagued by excessive costs and a high failure rate.[11]   Therefore, their popularity has faded rapidly as cost-efficiency and public safety became the paramount goals of the sentencing process in the present neo-conservative era. Intermediate sentencing is currently designed to be cost-effective and assure a high level of control. But, many of the structures it imposes on offenders parallel those evoked by the therapeutic community.

Discipline and Rehabilitation

Scholars have for some time been aware of the fact that discipline can have therapeutic effects. Lester stipulates that programs with a minimum of rules that are consistently enforced with uniformly applied penalties at an accepted level of severity will have maximal behavioral impact. He also asserts that program participants must be aware of the reasons for the rules, that the administrator of punishment should be a significant other and that penalties for infractions should consist of constructive tasks or the "natural consequences" of the rule violation.[12] These guidelines for therapeutic discipline form a substantial portion of the requisite logistics (i.e., bureaucratic necessities) of many emergent sentencing alternatives. They also form the basic structure (i.e., ground rules) for establishing and maintaining a rehabilitative program in a therapeutic community based upon the notion of management and control of behavior with parallel client insight-development, with respect to behavior, as a secondary goal.

The "self-help" approach is the dominant perspective of many therapeutic communities. Based primarily on the philosophy and methods of one particular support group, Alcoholics Anonymous (AA), the "self-help" model of behavior change stresses: (1) The import of support from others with similar problems and experiences; and, (2) the use of stigma to maintain and enhance changes in the desired direction. This latter element has been described as a "degradation ceremony."[13] It is believed to motivate functional behavior by keeping the offender salient of his/her past and thus using stigma to reconstruct past experiences that may then be used to motivate the offender's rejection of problematic behaviors and perceptions. Solidarity among group members is stressed in order to offset the negative impact of stigmatization, reinforce its positive uses, and help the offender gain self-knowledge.

This perspective is operationalized through clinical group therapies involving current and former deviants with similar problems. Groups such as Alcoholics Anonymous, Narcotics Anonymous, and Gamblers Anonymous meet regularly to share problems unique to their members, to universalize about their behaviors, to develop better and more socially acceptable coping and adjustment skills, and renew their commitment to following a conventional and functional lifestyle. The belief is that only those who have experienced particular phenomena can be fully empathic in a way that is of practical and clinical utility (i.e., encouraging insight into perceptual patterns and prediction of their outcomes). Because of this, self-help groups of this sort, although usually administratively supported by traditional social service and mental health agencies, are rarely led by "professional" counselors unless that person also has the same presenting problem. Since the current generation of alternative sentences rarely, if ever, encourages interactions between offenders, the integrative and social aspects of the self-help approach will be neglected in this discussion.

Attendance of such meetings is often required by both therapeutic communities and probation agencies. Additionally, both kinds of programs force offenders into insight development by helping them remain salient of their stigma, their role in creating it, and its import in their present and future decisions. Therapeutic communities do this through clinical groups as well as individual counseling sessions and routine interactions among members; hence, the idea of therapeutic communities as therapeutic milieux. The new generation of alternative sentences accomplishes very similar objectives through their frequent demand that electronic monitors be worn constantly as well as through surveillance procedures, random drug testing and similar control procedures.

LATENT FUNCTIONS OF THE CONTROL/PUNISHMENT APPROACH

While contact with current offenders is universally discouraged by probation or parole officers it is nonetheless inevitable as offender-clients queue up to pay fees, meet officials, and otherwise comply with the conditions of their release from custody. These interactions are not as thoroughly controlled as are those in therapeutic communities but, given the strict control-orientation of the new generation of alternative sentencing programs and their great readiness to revoke liberty, such interactions are likely to be far less criminogenic than in the past. Also, since offenders are generally of diverse backgrounds and value-orientations and are regularly subjected to the degradation of waiting on and answering to legal officials, many goals of the self-help model are nonetheless accomplished by the inadvertent arousal of salience of stigmatization. That is, an offender will have much in common with certain other offenders but is likely to reject many others in such a way as to motivate him/herself to avoid further acts that would exacerbate his/her contact with such undesirable individuals. This is a kind of "reality testing" that can also result in a secondary therapeutic gain.

Therapeutic communities are often very overt in their demand that clients follow a course of action based on the "act-as-if" model.[9] This model represents the clinical application of a synthesis of Festinger's cognitive dissonance theory and Bem's Self-Perception theory.[14] Old "street" self-images are deliberately undermined, if not overtly violated, by individualized behavioral mandates that are symbolic of the direction of behavior change that is sought for the client. The new generation of alternative sentences is more subtle in their demands for particular behaviors, demeanor and associations. Offender-clients are forced to maintain employment and clinical involvements, as well as to meet obligations to family, victims, and the community, while following strict curfews and permitting legal officials (or their appointees) to monitor other indicators of values and behavior. Programs stressing work, whether in the sense of a regimented "shock probation" boot camp or the less formal labor required through "community service," similarly act to pressure offenders into assuming a more acceptable self-concept and demeanor.

Various probation conditions can be used to compel an offender to behave in a manner to which he/she is not accustomed. Thus, they can be said to contain the basic rudiments of the "act-as-if" model of behavior change. This imposed behavior is, to some extent, in contradiction with the offender's self-image or values. Because of rigorous enforcement of probation conditions such self-violation can easily become defined as preferable to traditional incarceration and continued in spite of the dissonance it evokes. Seeking internal cohesion while attempting to avoid further formal sanctions, the offender must redefine him/herself. In so doing he/she gets the basic objective of the correctional regimen. Only when probation conditions are complete enough to force offenders to structure their lives in a socially acceptable manner and compliance is rigidly enforced will the desired results be gotten, however. Thus the punitive attitude taken by these new sentencing programs toward inappropriate behavior can be defined as a therapeutic method without alteration of its chief goal of enhancing public safety.

In therapeutic communities the client is forced to deal with reality in a functional way through deliberately structured confrontations with staff and peers as well as through individual and group counseling and didactic sessions.[10] In traditional community corrections the conditions under which the offender may remain at liberty are, or should be, explained in a fashion congruent with social reality.[15] Since the new genre of innovations in sentencing represents a more tightly controlled version of traditional forms, such explanations often must be given greater attention than previously because technological factors (e.g., electronic monitoring) are involved, technical revocations are more likely, and more detailed probation conditions are employed. The negotiation of probation conditions and their routine enforcement thus parallel the quasi-egalitarian counseling approach of the therapeutic community.

The outcome of these therapies is dependent on the successful insertion of planned and predictable routines and responsibilities into the offender's life. Therapeutic communities and similar facilities/programs designed to deal with offender populations allow their clients very little free time. Responsibility for enhancing one's social and vocational skills, maintaining the facility, providing for residents' daily needs, and getting treatment for individual problems occupy so much time that an occasional hour of leisure soon comes to be defined as a great luxury by residents.

The imposition of such structures on clients' time and activities has several desirable consequences. First, limits of this nature tend to reduce the likelihood that clients will become bored and seek "adventure" or attempt to vent their frustrations in too profligate a manner. Since they are so occupied by various activities throughout the day, it is not likely that they will dwell on minor irritations and difficulties that could provide rationalizations for unwise or anti-social behavioral choices. In addition, the constant involvement of the client in activities that are at least minimally monitored by members of the main-stream society reduces the likelihood of rebellion against rules imposed under the rationale of self-perception theory. Finally, by assuring the rarity of leisure, the salience of the subterranean values attached to free time is reduced and leisure becomes a reward, sui generis, rather than a source of boredom that motivates deviance in the attempt to find new adventures or relieve discomforts. Many punitive (e.g., community service) and financial conditions of probation serve much the same purpose in the newer alternatives to incarceration. Similarly, the incapacitating effect of home confinement puts limits of its own on the recreational opportunities available to offenders.

SUMMARY AND CONCLUSIONS

In this Chapter the writers have reviewed the manner in which two distinct sets of alternatives to incarceration have been implemented. The rehabilitative approach, as illustrated by the therapeutic community, sought to correct offending behavior by: (1) the imposition of functional routines and their inherent responsibilities on the offender, (2) the reduction of leisure time to an absolute minimum, (3) the recognition of social realities, choice-making, and personal responsibility for choice outcomes by the offender, (4) the alteration of self-image through the dissonance created by imposed behaviors and demeanor, (5) the use of stigma to motivate and maintain positive behavior changes; and, (6) the use of the insights of other offenders to identify and extinguish undesirable perceptual tendencies and behaviors.

It was noted in this chapter that the fundamental attributes of the therapeutic approach to corrections could be found in some of the newer, more punitive, programs. The imposition of structured routines on offender-clients is an inevitable logistical requirement of shock probation boot camps, house arrest, and intensively supervised probation. Such routines force the offender to lead a planned and predictable lifestyle and discourage impulsive actions. Such structure fosters the development of foresight and should act to increase the offender's "time horizon" and thus reduce his/her proclivity to crime.[4]

The new generation of alternative sentences is not designed to substantially reduce the offenders' leisure time, but shock probation boot camps keep this as a salient goal.[2]   And, community service can easily be employed by probation/parole officers to accomplish this goal.

The offender's distinction of his/her choice-making prerogatives is heightened by the imposition of structure on the offender's lifestyle. The strict enforcement of curfews, community service and other conditions of probation also force increased salience of choice-making and perceptual tendencies, and result in change based on the offender's own insight or understanding of his/her psychological or emotional processes. The immutability of social realities, such as the legal-bureaucratic system in which the offender finds him/herself enmeshed, can be driven home by the imposition of rigorously enforced probation itself. The same is true of individual responsibility for actions and their consequences.

The "act-as-if" model of rehabilitation is also surreptitiously invoked by these programs through the imposition of demands on the offender. Restitution, community service and the demand that other routine financial and familial responsibilities be met can serve to encourage the development of foresight, empathy and accountability in offenders. They also consume the offender's time and form a bond of involvement with the conventional society.[16]

The rigorous enforcement of employment requirements also tends to force offenders to maintain or enhance their ability to present themselves as socially acceptable persons.   This demand is much less rigorously enforced in community based programs than in residential ones for obvious reasons, but may still become an effective method for modifying the offender's self-image. This is especially true if employers, supervisors of community service work, and similarly placed individuals can be used as members of network teams to help probation officers monitor offender behaviors and self-presentation. The incorporation of vocational placement programs into intensive supervision and similar programs also would facilitate this end. Under the auspices of the new generation of alternatives to incarceration, it is conceivable that inclusion in such programs could become an earned reward for appropriate behavior, rather than an expected service of community corrections. Perhaps this is the direction in which such programs are moving.

Stigmatization occurs through the processes of arrest, trial, conviction and assignment to correctional supervision.   The use of electronic monitors increases awareness of stigma, as can the intensive surveillance of probationers in both its direct and indirect forms.   Probation officers need to better acquaint themselves with A.A.'s use of stigma to encourage and maintain positive behavior changes.   The addition of this approach to their arsenal of rehabilitative techniques, while valuable in itself, also will help to alleviate the role conflict associated with rehabilitative use of the offender's stigma and related dissonance.

NOTES

1.   Richard A. Ball and J. Robert Lilly. A Theoretical Examination of Home Incarceration, Federal Probation, Vol.   L, No. 1 (1986), pp. 17-24.

2.   Joan Petersilia. Expanding Options for Criminal Sentencing (Santa Monica, CA: Rand Corp, 1987).

3.   Edwin Zedlewski. Making Confinement Decisions, in Research in Brief (Washington, D.C.:   National Institute of Justice, Department of Justice, 1987).

4.   James Q. Wilson and Richard Herrnstein. Crime and Human Nature (New York: Simon and Schuster, 1985).

5.   James M. Byrne. Probation, in Crime File Study Guide (Washington, D.C.:   National Institute of Justice, U.S. Department of Justice, 1988).

6.   R. Martinson. What Works, The Public Interest, Vol. 35, (1974), pp. 22-54.

7.   Francis T. Cullen, Gregory A. Clark and John F. Wozniak.   Explaining The Get Tough Movement: Can the Public Be Blamed?, Federal Probation, Vol. XLIX, No. 2, (1985), pp. 16-24.

8.   Ronald P. Corbett, Jr. and Ellsworth A. Fersch. Home as Prison: The Use of House Arrest, Federal Probation, Vol. XLIX, No. 1, (1985), pp. 13-17.

9.   D. Kennard with J. Roberts. An Introduction to Therapeutic Communities (Boston, MA: Routlege & Kegan Paul, 1983).

10.   William Glasser. Reality Therapy (New York: Harper & Row, 1965).

11.   E. Kaufman and G. DeLeon. The Therapeutic Community: A Treatment Approach for Drug Abusers, in A. Schecter (ed.), Treatment Aspects of Drug Dependence (West Palm Beach, FL: C.R.C., 1978), pp. 83-98.

12.   David Lester. The Use of Punishment in Corrections and Crime Prevention, in S. Letman, L. French, H. Scott and D. Weichma (eds.),

Contemporary Issues in Corrections (New York: Pilgramage, Inc., 1981), pp. 1-6.

13.   H.M. Trice and P.M. Roman. Delabeling, Relabeling, and Alcoholics Anonymous, Social Problems, Vol. 17, No. 4, (1970), pp. 538-546.

14.   L.   Festinger. A Theory of Cognitive Dissonance (Stanford, CA: Stanford University Press, 1957); D.J. Bem. Self-Perception Theory, in L. Berkowitz (ed.), Advances in Experimental Social Psychology, Vol. 6 (New York: Academic Press, 1972), pp. 1-62.

15.   H. S. Sandhu. Community Corrections (Springfield, IL: Charles C. Thomas, 1981).

16.   Travis Hirschi. Causes of Delinquency (Berkeley, CA: University of California Press, 1969).

CHAPTER 4

ELECTRONIC MONITORING AS AN ALTERNATIVE SENTENCE

INTRODUCTION

Historically, correctional policies have reflected the values and concerns of society. Over time, the crucial central value expressed in all correctional policies was the idea that society was established in order to develop and maintain certain rights for individuals. This charged society with a mandate to exercise certain responsibilities toward the members of its collectivity. Explicitly, this meant extending protection to individuals from law breakers through the formation of certain criminal justice policies, and by the development of a criminal justice system to carry out these policies. Hence, social order and the preservation of health, safety and public order became key responsibilities of the criminal justice system.

Historically, however, these policies have not been unitary. Some scholars maintain that it is even problematic as to whether or not policies exist. This may be particularly true in the criminal justice field because of a number of reasons. First, instead of a unitary set of policies, what we seem to have is a an array of on-going decisions, retrospective analyses, implicit and explicit sets of principles, currents of case law and legalistic decision making, procedures and constraints, and an array of programs and services disguised as policy formulations. In total, a kind of schizophrenic array. In a second instance, it may be the case that the term criminal justice policies may be an oxymoron because of the overlapping and confounding nature of the policies that we do have. For example, at any one time we have a number of policies coexisting; some of which are fully developed; are evolving; and are (or are not), being implemented at various Federal, state, and local levels. And, finally, what we may think of as policies may be nothing more than the exercise of various kinds of discretionary actions at certain political and administrative levels by an assortment of political and administrative personalities who may be capriciously chasing one or more of any number of value orientations.

However, the general trends in policy-making which are clearly identifiable have been of two types. The first type are policies of a reformist-moralist nature. In these kinds of policies the explicit purpose seems to be tied-into the notion of upholding the morals and values of society. Some of these morals and values are enduring while others are in fashion at only one time or another. The emphasis with these policies, however, was on punishment and retribution.   Second, one can also find in the criminal justice arena policies which are usually referred to as   social welfare types of policies. These policies emphasize the ideal of rehabilitation of offenders and sees punishment as having only a minor impact on criminal behavior.

Gelman (after Duffee)[1] provides a model which provides a great deal of insight for understanding criminal justice policies, particularly with respect to the issues of goals and objectives. The sense of Duffee's conceptualizations in terms of general criminal justice policy objectives with respect to the issue of corrections follows in this manner:

> 1. Policy objectives which deal with restraint in the sense that correctional policies provide only for the incapacitation of the offender. With respect to restraint, incarceration and punishment are used as a means of retribution. The net effect is individual deterrence resulting in the protection of society as a secondary gain.

> 2. Policy objectives which are concerned with reform. In this case, there is little emphasis on the offender and a great deal of emphasis on the community. Any means necessary are used to change the offender without regard to his/her comfort.

> 3. Rehabilitation policy objectives wherein the efforts of correctional officers are seen as clinical or counseling activities that are directed at the behavior problems of the offenders. The emphasis is on behavioral change and the enhancement of self-esteem. Again, the outcome is expected to be conformity of the offender with respect to social norms.

> 4. A final way to view policy objectives is with respect to the concept of reintegration. This means that policy objectives need to foster a synthesis or a blending of the needs of the offender and the opportunities present in the community for rehabilitation via strategies which foster offender reintegration by enhancing opportunities for community interaction and involvement with offenders. This is often accomplished by networking with community social service elites and social service agencies and programs on behalf of offenders by the probationary staff.

If we look at general correctional policy objectives in more recent history, beginning with the onset of the 1960's, we can see some distinctive patterns being played out. For example, the decade of the 1960's was marked with rehabilitation efforts. Rehabilitative efforts intensified beginning with the passage of the Economic Opportunity Act of 1964 and other kinds of related social welfare legislation which followed. However, in the 1970's, and particularly as the Vietnam War began to wind down, the emphasis shifted toward concerns about public safety. Incarceration, which until the 1960's was the preferred response to crime, regained popularity. This policy shift resulted in a major institutional overcrowding problem. Federal and state prison populations more than doubled between 1972 to 1982. The response to the problem of overcrowding has typically been to build more prisons, but this does not appear to be economically or politically feasible.[2]

Although today incarceration is the preferred response, dissatisfaction with incarceration as the principal method of sanctioning criminal offenders has grown over the last two decades for a variety of reasons. First, the costs of incarceration and prison construction are staggering. To house, guard and provide for a single inmate, the estimated costs are between $10,000 - $30,000 per year. To put this cost structure into perspective, the upper end of this scale would pay for room, board and tuition for one year at most of the Ivy League colleges and universities in this country. Furthermore, each new bed space added to the prison system costs approximately $50,000.[3] Exacerbating the direct costs of imprisonment are indirect costs such as public and child welfare for the inmate's family and loss of taxes that would have been paid by the offender had he/she remained in the community. Second, the efficacy of institutional (and other) rehabilitative efforts have been brought into serious question in the last decade. Simultaneously, public opinion has shifted from concern with individual rights and welfare to the enhancement of public safety through improved control procedures. Finally, the tremendous growth in the number of incarcerated felons has resulted in prison overcrowding. The United States General Accounting Office reported in 1983 that the number of state and Federal prisoners grew by 24,000 to total 438,830 inmates at year's end.[4] This Office estimated that by 1990 there would be a total of 528,193 inmates within the United States prison system. This would occur at a time when its prison capacity is estimated to be 419,869. The U.S. Bureau of Justice Statistics (1985) reported that 26,618 prisoners were added to prison rolls in 1984 alone.[5] This brought the total growth to more than 134,000 inmates since 1980. This is a 40% increase over a four-year period. This trend has resulted in prison crowding, relief orders from the courts, and the implementation of early release mechanisms that undermine the incapacitation and deterrent functions of penal sanctions.[6] It has also caused many cities and counties to board-out their felons to other cities and counties that have more jail space. This necessity is causing extreme fiscal problems for many cities and counties.

The confluence of these two concerns - the costs of incarceration and hope for increased public safety through incapacitation - has resulted in the rapid growth of sentences more rigorous than traditional probation/parole but less costly than imprisonment. These alternatives to incarceration are designed to facilitate the management and control, rather than the rehabilitation, of offenders. Such alternative sentences can take a variety of forms and the unique situation of each offender can be taken into account in sentencing decisions.[3]

Two trends are at the root of the growth of electronic home confinement as a form of alternative sentencing: First, there is an increase in the prisoners held in the local jails, and second, there is an increase in correctional costs.

ALTERNATIVE SENTENCING

Overcrowded prisons, the apparent failure of the rehabilitative ideal, fiscal pressures, an ever-increasing crime rate and similar exigencies set the socio-political stage   for a new generation of sanctions intermediate between incarceration and the cursory supervision of traditional community corrections. These alternatives to incarceration are currently used as a control-oriented approach to penal sanctions that are less costly but more incapacitating than traditional methods of community supervision.

Five rationales for the use of alternative sentences have been developed that provide a basis for both program design and evaluation:

> 1. If the offender is held accountable for his crimes in the community where they were committed, then restitution can be provided if appropriate;

> 2. Use of a genuine deterrent by punishing the offender in the community may be successful because more can be done with existing resources while simultaneously reducing the costs per offender;

> 3. Rehabilitation is more successful when the community plays a part in the outcome and the offenders' ties to family and employers remain intact;

4. Non-violent offenders can avoid the criminogenic learning and socialization/acculturation influences of the prison subculture;

5. Finally, it is not possible to bestow a prison sentence upon every offender and expect to have enough prison space. Overcrowding can and has resulted in the premature release of serious offenders so as to free space for other, often less dangerous, convicts.[7]

The potential uses of electronic monitoring as an alternative are pretrial diversion, weekend sentences, work release, use with juveniles, and for medical reasons such as pregnancy, AIDS, and mental, physical, or emotional handicaps. There is, however, also the potential for abuse of this technology. For example, using it with individuals who would be granted community supervision anyway, using it for excessively long durations, negotiating pleas without consideration of public safety, using it as a quick fix for the overcrowding problem, and/or using it with inappropriate offenders.[2]

ELECTRONICALLY MONITORED HOME CONFINEMENT

Electronically monitored home confinement (EM) is a supervisory method used as an alternative to jail or prison. It is implemented as a condition or sanction of probation or parole. Although EM uses modern technology to assure that an offender complies with the temporal restrictions of his/her release from custody, the concept of electronic monitoring was developed as early as 1919.[2]

There are three levels of home confinement. The first, which is the least severe, is the curfew. This is a type of home confinement that requires the client to stay in his/her residence during a limited period of time, usually at night. The second type of home confinement is home detention. With this remedy, the offender is required to remain in his/her residence at all times, except for employment, education, medical or mental health treatment, or any other type of authorized leave. The third type is the most severe. It is the incarceration at home, or, in reality, house arrest. The client is to remain in the residence at all times with few exceptions such as religious services or medical treatment.[8]

Nationally, in 1987 there were 821 offenders in 21 states being monitored electronically. In 1988 the number of offenders being electronically monitored increased to 2,300 in 33 states. In both 1987 and 1988 men were primarily monitored. For example, only 10.2% of monitored offenders in 1987 were females. Similarly, in 1988   12.7% of the offenders being monitored were females. In 1987 the majority of the offenses committed by offenders being electronically monitored were DWI's and other major traffic offenses. But in 1988, EM was increasingly used to monitor the perpetrators of more serious offenses including property crimes and drug offenses.[8] This trend continues today.

Electronic monitoring systems are divided into two broad categories: Those that operate with a telephone and those that do not require a telephone. In the first category, operating with telephones, there is a continuous signaling system which constantly monitors the offender. A more common sub-type also requires a telephone. With this system the telephone is a programmed-contact system that randomly calls the offender and verifies his or her presence at the time of the call. The second category does not require telecommunications; rather, it relies on radio signals. The monitor, usually a private contractor, uses a car with a monitoring receiver to oversee compliance instead of a computer. The transmitter is attached to the offender, and when the officer drives by the residence being monitored he/she is able to detect if the person being monitored is inside the residence or not. There is also another type of radio signal system that operates similarly to continuous telephone signaling, but uses radio transmitters.[2]   In 1987 and 1988, nationwide, 56% of the offenders were monitored using continuously signaling equipment while 42% were monitored randomly, using programmed contact devices.[8]

Although there are now numerous types of continuous and random electronic monitoring devices in operation today, the most effective is one of the continuous type where a monitoring transmitter is attached to the offenders' ankle, and a monitoring receiver attached to the telephone, so that a break in the signal between the monitoring transmitter and receiver alerts the monitoring office of curfew violations. Random electronic monitoring, as the name implies, does not continually monitor the offender but rather verifies that the offender is at home through either random contact by telephone or telephone contact at pre-specified times during the day. Random electronic monitoring devices may also utilize some type of voice, picture, or transmitter verification.

Persons placed on home confinement are usually non-violent or first offenders who are generally not considered a threat to society, but are still in need of supervision.   Courts and parole boards/departments are placing these offenders on EM as a condition or sanction of their probation or parole. The usual   amount of time a probationer or parolee must serve on EM is 30 to 90 days.

When an offender reports to his/her probation or parole officer, he/she must obtain a weekly schedule which specifies what times during the day the offender may be away from his/her residence for work, treatment (psychological, alcohol, drug), medical, or religious reasons. If the person is not at their residence according to the time schedule, a violation is reported and the probation or parole officer is notified. If a serious violation occurs or a number of minor violations occur, the offender's probation or parole can be revoked and the offender sent to prison in the case of probation, or returned to prison in the case of parole.

Electronic monitoring is felt to be constitutionally permissible as it is now used because: (1) the person under scrutiny is a convicted criminal and therefore has a lower expectation of privacy than the normal citizen; and, (2) participation in the program is usually voluntary, therefore the offender knows and accepts all conditions of the program before he/she is "hooked-up" to EM.[6]

The curfew restrictions and other conditions of probation, parole, and other diversionary programs are considered valid as long as they are reasonably related to rehabilitation of the individual and/or to the protection of society. When an offender volunteers, he or she denotes consent and this provides a valid wavier of rights. Electronic monitoring does not violate the Fourth Amendment Constitutional right against unreasonable search and seizures because the device is used to determine that the offender is confined to his or her residence, not to determine what he or she is doing in the home. There is no violation of the Fifth Amendment right against self-incrimination because the incrimination is physical and not testimonial. It is a humane alternative to incarceration, therefore it is not cruel and unusual punishment. Electronic monitoring does not intercept any verbal or oral communication so it does not violate Federal Law (e.g. Title III of the Omnibus Crime Control and Safe Streets Act of 1968). Each state must determine if there are existing statutes authorizing, limiting or prohibiting electronic monitoring.[2]

Collectively, these types of electronically monitoring programs helped supervise over 2,300 offenders nationally. This is three times the number of people monitored one year earlier. The current trend in such programs appears to be a gradual expansion to include offenders at higher risk levels.[9] It is expected that we will see a greater use of electronic monitoring with higher risk offenders. The same reasons that are giving impetus for the use of EM with this group of offenders gave impetus for the use of electronic monitoring in the first place: Monetary costs and prison over-crowding. The implications of the use of EM with higher risk offenders are very problematic and some examples of the tragic consequences of its use with these types of offenders are just now being reported in the media.

Due to the problems associated with offenders housed in county jails while awaiting transfer to penitentiaries, brief mention should be made of the fact that many of the arguments used in favor of increased use of EM in lieu of prison also apply to the increased use of EM in lieu of jail. For example, the costs of jailing offenders are considerably higher than those of EM. The average daily cost of housing an offender in jail is estimated to be between $40 and $56 per day, depending upon the agency and the type of facility in question. Electronic monitoring, on the other hand, has an average daily costs of $7 to $14 per offender per day, depending upon whether the electronic monitoring equipment is purchased or leased, or the service is contracted.[3]

If used selectively, EM as well as other alternatives to incarceration such as Client Specific Planning, advocated by the National Center on Institutions and Alternatives, have the potential to have a leveling effect on prison and/or jail populations. That is, to maintain them at their current levels. There is also some possibility of actually reducing them over time. As already noted, EM along with other alternative sentencing and parole programs have the potential for reducing the rate of prison expansion in the future, the need for new construction, and the size of the existing imprisoned population. They can also serve to improve the efficacy of rehabilitation under community supervision.

Electronic monitoring, as an alternative sentencing or parole program, can be responsive to the needs of the criminal justice system and the needs of individual offenders because of its flexibility. Individual offenders can be placed on EM at any time (e.g., in lieu of jail, after a short-term in jail, in lieu of prison, after a prison term, or as a condition of probation or parole). It can also be used for different types of offenders, accommodate various schedules for work and clinical activity, and special cases; e.g., offenders who are mentally retarded, terminally ill, elderly, or stricken with AIDS.[3]

Finally, EM programs are relatively easy to implement and the EM conditions and sanctions imposed on the offenders are easily understood by them. Electronic monitoring does not require any new facilities or personnel (when technical services are provided by contractors) and can be used at minimal expense relative to prison costs. In addition, should the offender violate his/her conditions of EM, they can be removed quickly from the community.[3]

Electronic monitoring should not be viewed and/or used as a substitute for traditional probation or parole supervision. Computers and transmitters should not replace the human contact needed for proper supervision. It appears to be the case that electronic monitoring can serve as a punishment. But, it is problematic as to whether or not it contributes to the rehabilitation of offenders. In later Chapters the authors present a description and the results of a study directed at the question of the effectiveness of the use of EM with parolees and probationers on house arrest. In the qualified judgment of the writers, in certain significant areas, the use of EM makes a difference. To date, however, they know of no scientific evidence demonstrating that criminal activity is reduced while electronic monitoring is being utilized or after the use of the technology with offenders. To date the evidence suggests that when properly utilized, EM provides another alternative to incarceration, but nothing else. Electronic monitoring has been used with both probationers and parolees. Preliminary data indicate it to be relatively successful in reducing revocations for new crimes, but its impact on the psychological welfare of offenders and members of their households have not been thoroughly explored. For example, Schmidt found that for the most part, EM programs which had reported a variety of problems associated with EM such as the need for proper training, family adjustment difficulties, equipment malfunctions, and poor telephone lines or wires were able to resolve them.[8]

Later in this book the writers also describe, from their study, the effects of EM upon the family environments of offenders. In a different aspect, Friel, Vaughn, and del Carmen looked at the use of electronic monitoring by ten programs. Their information was gathered by interviews and questionnaires, and also included interviews of 55 offenders exiting from EM programs concerning behavioral effects. They found that a majority of the agencies in their study started to use EM because of overcrowding of jails and prisons. The agencies had learned of the technology by attending professional meetings, through visits by vendors, or by word of mouth. Generally, state and local governments bought the equipment for these agencies, and the offenders placed on EM were charged a daily fee, usually of $7.00.[2]

Friel, Vaughn, and del Carmen also reported that the average number of offenders in the ten programs they studied ranged from 4 to 20 per month, with an average duration between 1 and 2 months. The primary problem they reported in their study was with the equipment itself. The benefits reported were that electronic monitoring was a humane yet restrictive alternative to jail or prison. Offenders in the EM programs had to work, and, therefore, paid fines and restitution, supported their families, paid taxes, and lived a relatively normal life. Most of the offenders did not mind being monitored, but found curfew to be difficult. They reported that their peer group relations changed mainly because of the curfew. They became more dependent on their family and friends because they were home-bound. They also became more domestic. The majority reported that the device they had to wear was not socially embarrassing and some even used it as an excuse for not doing something or going somewhere. They reported being healthier and wealthier and the experience was generally defined as rewarding.[2]

Goss also found the programs to be useful in easing the transition from the institution to the community. He further found that agencies utilizing EM found relief from the population increase while still punishing and controlling offenders. Goss also reported that most programs require the offender to be employed, thereby allowing for the offender to be able to pay part of the cost.[10]

Schmidt, in a national survey, found that the EM structures were set up differently in each state. She reported that the state departments of corrections, local courts, sheriff's departments, local departments of correction, or private agencies were used to different degrees in each state.[8]

ADULT PROBATION

Probation is normally seen as a form of community supervision in which the offender contractually surrenders certain freedoms and submits to various conditions in exchange for being permitted to remain at liberty in the community. Probation departments are partially funded by the state, but decision-making remains firmly grounded at the local level. Probation departments are under the direct control of the local judiciary which allows them great flexibility in customizing the conditions of release to the needs of both the community and the particular offender.[11]

Probation is well-suited to the needs of and risks posed by non-violent offenders who do not yet have an extensive criminal history. It allows the convicted offender to live normally within the community, pay taxes, support dependents and make restitution for his/her crime, instead of being imprisoned. The offender is assigned to a probation officer and must comply with the rules and conditions imposed by the court. The sentencing court may also impose probation fees, court costs, fines, court-appointed attorney fees, and restitution fees.[11]

Probation officers classify offenders based on risk scores (risk scales) according to the level of supervision they require - minimal, normal, and intensive. The probationers' clinical and vocational needs are assessed at the same time. Thus a continuum of incapacitation, and implicitly punishment, is established within each probation department's caseload. Electronic monitoring is generally considered to be intermediate between intensive supervision in the community and incarceration.[12]

After the offender has gone through the probation department's intake process and has been assigned to an officer, the offender then fills out a number of forms for informational purposes. This information is used to assess the offender's needs as well as the nature and severity of the risks that the offender may pose to others and to the community-at-large. Clients are rated on criteria which estimate risks, offenders needs and/or status, and also assesses direct surveillance, rehabilitative, and classification techniques used for the offender.[12]

Risk assessments evaluate the offender on past behavior or contact with the criminal justice system, stability of ties to the community, age, and any substance abuse or psycho-social dysfunctions. A high assessment score indicates a need for more intensive supervision. In short, the offender is rated on a risk assessment scale in order to enhance public protection.[11]

Specific conditions, which are applied to each offender, can be modified during the course of a probated sentence. Failure to submit to any of these conditions can result in the placement of sanctions (additional conditions of probation) or revocation of probation. The offender would, in the case of sanctions, remain in the community and have to adhere to the original conditions of probation plus the additional conditions imposed as sanctions, or in the case of revocation serve the remainder of his/her sentence in prison.[12]

Because their training is usually oriented more toward rehabilitation than law enforcement, and because most probation officers seem to be more philosophically in tune with rehabilitative rather than retributive approaches. Therefore, they are often reluctant to revoke an offender's liberty for minor technical violations. Lack of available prison space can also make revocation unfeasible in many cases. They are more often than not inclined to use available community social service resources to ensure the success of their caseloads.[3] That is, probation officers will generally seek to have additional sanctions imposed on violators prior to revoking their probation.

Currently, one of the best administrative/programmatic locations for the use of electronic monitoring lies in "intensive supervision probation" programs (hereafter referred to as ISP). These types of programs are in vogue in many probationary departments. The primary purpose of intensive service programs is to act as a diversion from incarceration. The program is designed to provide a higher level of supervision then usual so as to produce positive changes in high risk probationers while more effectively insuring public safety. Offenders are placed on intensive supervision as a method of diversion from incarceration. This decision is made at the initial stage when the decision to incarcerate is first presented in court or can be imposed as a sanction. Within intensive supervision programs per se, it is also possible to structure levels of intensive supervision by using various types of rating systems or risk scales, i.e., a kind of case classification system. This is an approach that has been historically used in mental health agencies and programs and is analogous to the case management approach. In the Chapter that follows, conceptualization and descriptions concerning the applicability and use of case management methods with parolees and probationers on electronic monitoring will be discussed.

In any case, the intensive supervision approach allows probation officers to focus their control and rehabilitative efforts in a more selective and less-random way. If employed as a sanction it is generally imposed on probationers on regular probation who have violated their condition(s) of probation. Offenders who do well under ISP are then placed on regular probation. Offenders who are unable to comply with ISP conditions then become candidates for electronic monitoring so long as they pose no apparent threat to the community.

Offenders who are eligible for ISP include persons that have:

> 1. Been considered for shock probation;
>
> 2. A current felony probationary sentence and have been charged with a violation of probation;
>
> 3. A prior commitment to jail or prison;
>
> 4. Chronic unemployment problems;
>
> 5. Prior felony convictions;
>
> 6. Documented chemical abuse problems;
>
> 7. Documented limited mental capacity, mental retardation, or learning disabilities;
>
> 8. Been charged with serious offenses.[12]

Intensive supervision programs are often imposed for a period of one year. Offenders on ISP usually report at least twice a month on specified days as compared to once a month for those offenders who are on regular probation.

After a prescribed period of time, probation is reassessed and the offender is placed on regular probation if he or she has successfully completed ISP. Intensive supervision can, however, be extended for an additional period should any problems remain unresolved. The vast majority of offenders who have been placed on EM are probationers who have been placed originally on ISP and who have violated their conditions of release.[12]

SUMMARY AND CONCLUSIONS

In summary, even though correctional policies seem to be somewhat problematic in our society, correctional policies have tended to reflect, at one time or another, the ebb and flow of popular and political opinions and concerns about incarceration. These concerns and opinions have centered about incarceration as an opportunity for punishment and/or retribution or incarceration as an opportunity for rehabilitation. These value sets are now over-shadowed because of more pragmatic concerns about the economics of prisonization. It does appear that, regardless of one's value orientation about the issue of incarceration, we cannot simply build more prisons and furnish more prisons beds. The problems stemming from incarceration and the advantages of EM for non-violent offenders jointly provide an opportunity for improving community corrections. Prison is expensive, decreases chances of reintegration into society, reinforces criminal acculturation and socialization, provides opportunities for learning more sophisticated criminal techniques, creates racial divisions, and promotes gang violence and sexual assaults. In short, it is not a realistic response to all forms of crime.[13] In the opinion of the authors, these arguments appear to be strong social-psychological and political justifications for the use of EM.

Some of the advantages of the use of EM are that it is cost effective in that it saves states yearly prison housing costs. These cost now average between $10,000 - $15,000 per year. It also reduces the pressure to build new prisons. New prison construction now averages approximately $50,000.per bed.[3] The estimated daily cost per EM unit per day for purchase ranges from $1.29 to $9.04; from $0.95 to $7.00 per day for a lease-purchase agreement; and, from $1.19 to $7.00 per day to lease.[2] From the perspective of the writers, these data seem to argue well in terms of economic and business rationalizations for the use of this technology.

However, administrators must consider the opportunity costs when using alternatives such as electronic monitoring. The time and equipment costs of EM are likely to mean the sacrifice of other possible programs. That is to say, a consideration must be given to the trade-offs that society must be willing to consider in adopting the technology. These trade-offs also have to do with issues of freedom and authority in the humanistic sense. For example, the issue of Constitutional rights have not been entirely explored and considered. The use of electronic monitoring is in its judicial infancy with respect to this issue. Another humanistic issue concerns the use of all forms of behavioral management approaches per se. Electronic monitoring and the technology it spawns for purposes of intruding into the life space of offenders carries implications for the possibility of intrusion into the life spaces of all of us.

Furthermore, it is too early to determine the actual cost efficiency of the technology relative to other sorts of programs currently available in probationary departments. There are trade-offs in cost benefit terms, but it seems to be neither humanistically nor economically beneficial to hold people in jail or prison who need not be there. At least, EM/ISP makes offenders more accountable to their supervising officers. This last point is perhaps the most telling argument in favor of the use of EM.

NOTES

1.   Sheldon R. Gelman. Correctional Policies: Evolving Trends, in Albert R. Roberts (ed.), Social Work in Juvenile and Criminal Justice Settings (Springfield, IL.: Charles C. Thomas Publisher, 1983).

2.   Charles M. Friel, Joseph B. Vaughn, and Rolando del Carmen. Electronic Monitoring and Correctional Policy: The Technology and Its Application, Research Report (Washington, D.C: National Institute of Justice, U.S. Department of Justice, 1987).

3.   Joan Petersilia. House Arrest, in Crime File Study Guide (Washington, D.C.: National Institute of Justice, U.S. Department of Justice, 1988).

4.   United States General Accounting Office (1984).

5.   U.S. Bureau of Justice Statistics (1985).

6.   Thomas G. Blomberg, Gordon P. Waldo, and Lisa C. Burcroff. Home Confinement and Electronic Surveillance, in Belinda R. McCarthy (ed.), Intermediate Punishments: Intensive Supervision, Home Confinement and Electronic Surveillance (Monsey, NY: Willow Tree Press, 1987).

7.   Texas Board of Pardons and Parole Annual Statistical Report (1987).

8.   Annesley K. Schmidt. Electronic Monitoring of Offenders Increases, in NIJ Reports (Washington, D.C.: National Institute of Justice, Office of Justice Programs, U.S. Department of Justice, No. 212 (1989), pp. 2-5.

9.   Annesley K. Schmidt and Christine E. Curtis. Electronic Monitors, in Belinda R. McCarthy (ed.), Intermediate Punishments: Intensive Supervision, Home Confinement and Electronic Surveillance (Monsey, NY: Willow Tree Press, 1987).

10.   M. Goss. Electronic Monitoring: The Missing Link for Successful House Arrest, Corrections Today, Vol. 51, No. 4 (1989), pp. 106-110.

11.   Richard C. Grinter. Electronic Monitoring of Serious Offenders in Texas, Journal of Offender Monitoring, Vol. 2, No. 4 (1989), pp. 1-14.

12.   Denton County Court Services, Adult and Juvenile Probation Department. Intensive Supervision Probationer's Guide (Denton, TX: Denton County Court Services, Adult and Juvenile Probation Department, 1987).

13.   N. Arrigona and T. Fabelo. Probation and Prison Populations in Texas: Potential Diversions and Hardening of Prison Population, in Criminal Justice Policy Council Interim Report to the 71st Texas House of Representatives (Austin, TX: Criminal Justice Policy Council, 1989).

CHAPTER 5

COUNSELING OFFENDERS ON ELECTRONIC MONITORING:
A CASE MANAGEMENT APPROACH

INTRODUCTION

Casemanagement has increasingly become the counseling method of choice of clinical practitioners who work with clients that have a multiplicity of social, psychological and behavioral problems. Casemanagement has become a widespread treatment approach in state and local mental health agencies. In these kinds of agencies the use of casemanagement has been particularly appropriate in counseling chronically mentally disabled persons in community-based (deinstitutionalized) settings.

Criminal offenders mirror the chronically mentally disabled in that they also have a multiplicity of severe and persistent social and psychological disorders and, in some cases, pathologies. These problems make it extremely difficult for them to function in a responsible and competent manner with respect to their individual, family, group and community relationships.

The counseling goals for all categories of clients in deinstitutionalized settings, whether we are discussing the chronically mentally disabled or the parolee or probationer "doing time at home" on electronic monitoring, are the same: rehabilitation of the client/offender (change and/or modification of personal behavior), and reintegration into the community in particular and into the larger society in general (assumption and demonstration of normative, i.e., appropriate social roles and responsibilities).

The purpose of this Chapter is to present the reader with a description and an elaboration of the use of casemanagement as a preferred method for counseling parolees and probationers who are being electronically monitored while under house arrest.

CASEMANAGEMENT

With respect to the issue of the use of casemanagement as a method for counseling parolees and probationers on electronic monitoring as discussed in this Chapter, the term casemanagement will refer to two distinctive processes: the casemanager generalist function, and the casemanager counselor function.

The Casemanager Generalist

The casemanager as a generalist directs his or her counseling energies toward the external world of the parolee or probationer. This can be thought of as a kind of meso- or macro-level counseling approach which is characterized by the casemanager acting on behalf of the client in relation to a variety of social systems and social institutions of various types and sizes. Specifically, in this role the casemanager is principally interested in linking the parolee or probationer with the wide array of social welfare and human services from which he or she may obtain appropriate resources to aid in personal rehabilitation and reintegration into society. In this sense, the casemanager as generalist is interested in linking the parolee or probationer with concrete services, such as: social welfare income maintenance programs; food, clothing, and housing assistance programs; physical, rehabilitative, vocational and educational training programs; and, health promotion, treatment and maintenance programs. In addition, the casemanager as generalist also strives to link the parolee or probationer with appropriate community based mental health programs. Such programs may include: public and private (non-profit) individual, family, and group mental health, psychotherapy, and counseling services; support groups; and, various peer-counseling and self-recovery programs which are of particular value to the parolee and probationer and his/her family, e.g., AA, AL-ANON, OPEN, I Am Victorious, Inc., etc. These kinds of activities generally involve the casemanager as generalist in a broad range of "networking" or professional liaison activities with other professional helping persons and with community agencies. Thus, the casemanager as generalist must have a good awareness of the number and types of human service and social welfare service agencies in his or her community. He or she must also understand the structure, function and services available via the programs in these agencies.

The casemanager generalist must also have a diagnostic understanding of the particular rehabilitative and reintegration needs of his/her clients, their motivation for rehabilitation and reintegration, and the quality and levels of their physical, intellectual, educational and emotional capacities that might be brought to bear on the efforts toward rehabilitation and reintegration. This is a necessary condition in order to make a good therapeutic match between the parolee or probationer and the specific agency program or service, or perhaps, the specific individual or type of service personnel that the parolee or probationer may need via referral. It is this type of role, that most probation officers are accustommed to performing.

The Casemanager Counselor

In contrast to the casemanager as generalist, the casemanager as counselor directs his or her professional energies toward the internal, i.e., psychological world, of the parolee or probationer on electronic monitoring. The focus of the counseling effort here is upon intrinsic aspects of the persona. It is a counseling approach which is directed at the cognitive, affective and behavioral domains of these clients. The goals of rehabilitation and reintegration of parolees and probationers can, ultimately, only be accomplished in a full sense if parolees and probationers, through the vehicle of the counseling process, obtain insight and understanding of their cognitive, affective and behavioral functioning. And, further, if the counseling process challenges them to change or modify distorted or problematic aspects of these areas of their functioning.

The casemanager as generalist and the casemanager as counselor must not be viewed as dichotomies or as separate areas for casemanagement activity. This is because the parolee or probationer on electronic monitoring, like other types of persons with problems in social or psychological functioning, or, anyone, for that matter, inhabits, simultaneously, both an external social world and an internal psychological world. The caveat, then, is that professional casemanagement activities which are directed at the rehabilitation and reintegration of parolees and probationers on electronic monitoring must include parallel and, often, simultaneous casemanagement generalist and casemanagement counselor activities. Probation officers may perform crisis intervention or seize unique opportunities to counsel clients but the primary therapist is best obtained from the mental health system.

Theoretical Base

A number of therapeutic approaches exist which contain viable methods for counseling with this population via the casemanager as generalist or the casemanager as counselor roles. In the opinion of the writers, the degree and extent of social and psychological disorders and pathologies that one is likely to encounter in a cohort group of parolees and probationers on house arrest are not likely to be so severe as to preclude virtually any approach ranging from supportive and sustaining strategies through psychotherapies of various sorts. There may be, however, some specific treatment methods of choice with this group.   The authors believe that this may be accurate with respect to what has been variously described in the clinical and counseling literature as the cognitive-behavior theory method. The argument may be made in the following way: electronic monitoring and home confinement, because of the technological aspects of the monitoring process per se, which function to externally manage, direct, compel, and reward appropriate behaviors by parolees and probationers, may be viewed as a particularistic type of behavioral treatment approach. The externalization aspects of behavioral methods implicit in this approach can be naturally combined in clinical practice with cognitive methods which result in a hybrid approach generally referred to in the literature as the cognitive-behavioral treatment method. The two methods have a natural counseling complimentority because, in combination, they are directed toward the external and internal dimensions of the client and of his or her problems. The approach is, sui generis, psychosocial. In addition, there is also some research evidence to suggest that such combined approaches may be effective with clients in the criminal justice system and, particularly, with delinquents. [1]

To further understand this approach, one needs to explore its theoretical roots and consider some of its contemporary definitions. The writers believe that the general theoretical formulations of this approach originated with Adler as a consequence of certain disagreements that he had with Freud about psychological development. In Adler's "Individual Psychology", greater importance was attached to the influence of the environment, life style, and distorted attitudes and behaviors as factors in personality development rather than, for example, certain personality factors such as the libido and the unconscious.[2] Since Adler, and in essentially a revisionistic fashion, the original theoretical formulations in his approach have served to sprout a constellation of related theoretical notions; each, in many cases, identified by its originator.

The cognitive-behavioral approach for generalist or generalist-counselor casemanagers was captured by Werner in this way: "A cognitive approach holds that the principle determinant of emotions, motives, and behavior is an individual's thinking which is a conscious process." (P. 91).[3] More definitively, for Lazarus, this approach derives from learning principles, and, particularly, from social learning, cognitive processes, and behavioral principles which appear to be experimentally related to how and why individuals learn and unlearn adaptive and maladaptive behaviors. (P. 4).[4] In short, the method contains a number of concepts concerning the nature of the therapeutic relationship, the nature of personality development, and the nature of personality change which supply the elements for an effective strategy that can be used by casemanagers as generalists or as counselors who wish to work effectively with probationers and parolees on electronic monitoring and home arrest.

Later in this Chapter the writers will describe the use of the casemanager as generalist and the casemanager as counselor process with respect to working with parolees and probationers on electronic monitoring and will present some examples. Before engaging in any analysis of casemanagement activities, however, it is important for the reader to explore and understand two issues: the nature of the therapeutic relationship; and, the psychosocial assessment or diagnosis process.

THE THERAPEUTIC RELATIONSHIP

Unless the casemanager is able to establish a therapeutic relationship with the parolee or probationer probably very little will be accomplished in relation to moving in a positive direction in reference to the rehabilitation and reintegration goals that had been established for these clients. The validity of this point has been well established in clinical literature across a variety of disciplinary fields and client types.[5]

Terms such as therapeutic relationship, supportive and sustaining relationships, rapport, etc., refer to a set of interpersonal values which are an essential part of the personal dynamics of successful counselors. Across the literature, this set of interpersonal values have been most clearly identified with the work of Carl Rogers. Over time, they have been referred to as the "core conditions" of positive outcomes in counseling. (Pp.: 19-64).[6]

This writers prefer to refer to counselors who have some good measure of these kinds of characteristics as "empathetic counselors". Empathetic counselors manifest their acceptance, respect and positive regard for clients through the mechanism of their counseling service delivery. That is to say, their interpersonal values are behaviorally manifested in their interpersonal counseling encounters with the client. In short, empathetic counselors translate acceptance, affirmation and respect in the interpersonal counseling relationship with the clients into counseling or treatment techniques.

CORE CONDITIONS FOR EMPATHETIC CASEMANAGERS

Although Rogers identified a number of core conditions that he believed to be associated with positive therapeutic outcomes in therapy, in the opinion of these writers four, in particular, are most useful for casemanagers who work with parolees and probationers on electronic monitoring. These conditions are: genuineness, congruence, unconditional positive regard, and empathetic understanding.

Genuineness has to do with the nature of self-disclosure and refers to the ability of the counselor to be an open, direct and candid communicator. Authentic counselors are those who are not pedantic, pedagogical, or "phony". For the successful casemanager it means to say it clearly and unambiguously. Hepworth and Larsen (while defining it as "authenticity") describe it in this fashion: "Authenticity involves the practitioner's sharing of self by relating in a natural, sincere, spontaneous, open, and genuine manner. Being authentic, or genuine, involves relating personally so that expressions are spontaneous rather than contrived." (P. 424).[7]

Congruence refers to the degree of interface or match between the counselor's thoughts, feelings, expressions, affect and body language and his or her communication to the client. The successful casemanager projects a singular message to the parolee or probationer both verbally and non-verbally. His or her verbalizations are not paradoxical or confused or negated by non-verbal messages (such as body language or facial expressions) which implicitly convey a contrary message. Keefe and Maypole put it this way:

> Several nonverbal behaviors of communicating empathy are related to a positive outcome of the helping relationship when they are congruent with corresponding verbal respons-es - that is, when practitioner's feelings and thoughts are in harmony with their words, tone of voice, facial expression, movements, and gestures. (P. 71). [8]

Unconditional positive regard is an additional value of successful casemanagers. For Meador (interpreting Rogers) unconditional positive regard meant:

> . . . a non-possessive caring or an acceptance of his individu-ality . . . This attitude comes in part from the therapist's trust in the inner wisdom of the actualizing processes in the client, and in his belief that the client will discover for himself the resources and directions his growth will take. (P. 127). [9]

Consistent with Roger's theoretical formulations, unconditional positive regard means acceptance of the person. It is an acceptance of the what the Quakers refer to as: "that of God in every man". For some clinicians acceptance of the person in the therapeutic relationship means acceptance of the person but not necessarily approval of the behavior. A therapeutic mid-course would be the stance of a non-judgmental view of the behavior. This is a condition which may consciously be supportable but which is difficult to maintain in the unconscious sense because, for example, it is difficult not to both dislike the murder and the murderer. In terms of the casemanager in criminal justice settings, perhaps Biestek's definition of the term "acceptance" comes closest to being a realistic commandment for successful casemanagement.

> Acceptance is a principle of action wherein the caseworker perceives and deals with the client as he really is, including his strengths and weaknesses, his congenial and uncongenial qualities, his positive and negative feelings, his constructive and destructive attitudes and behavior, maintaining all the while a sense of the client's innate dignity and personal worth. Acceptance does not mean approval of deviant attitudes or behavior. The objective of acceptance is not 'the good' but 'the real,'. . . (P. 72).[10]

With respect to the issue of counseling with probationers and parolees, the writers believe that the conditions of empathetic counseling include acceptance of the person but not acceptance of the behavior nor approval of the behavior. This point must be clearly noted since parolees and probationers, by contrast with most types of traditional, i.e., voluntary clients seeking counseling services, are persons who have violated criminal laws. This is the overarching personal and situational dynamic with respect to parolees and probationers on electronic monitoring that must be understood.

Empathetic Functioning

This concept refers to the ability of the counselor to achieve an empathetic understanding of the client's personal frame of reference. Rogers (1957) sums it up this way:

> The fifth condition is that the therapist is experiencing an accurate, empathic understanding of the client's awareness of his own experience. To sense the client's private world as if it were your own, but without ever losing the 'as if' quality - this is empathy, and this seems essential to therapy. To sense the client's anger, fear, or confusion as if it were your own, yet without your own anger, fear, or confusion getting bound up in it. . . (P. 99).[11]

For the successful casemanager working with probationers and parolees it means that he or she must be able to "tune in" and become aware of their problems and to do this in a sensitive manner while not trampling on the meanings for the clients that are contained within their problems and in their expressions of feelings.

Empathetic functioning also means that the casemanager must respond in an appropriate professional manner by not "playing into" or getting "caught up" in the problems of the client. It also means that the casemanager, particularly with this population, must become aware of his or her own "psychological softspots", i.e., his or her needs, wishes, desires, insecurities, because these clients may wish to exploit these softspots in an attempt to manipulate or control the casemanager. In short, it means that the casemanager tries to understand what it must be like to "walk in the shoes of the probationer or parolee" but, at the same time, he or she must be able to establish appropriate social and psychological distance or space between these clients and their problems and the casemanager's own needs, wishes, desires, and insecurities.

Allegorically speaking, when his or her parolees or probationers hurt emotionally, the casemanager must not cry. An essential question to ask here is: "whose needs are being met"? It is all too easy to take the less conflictive course and "say yes" when we should say "no"; or to give the overly-optimistic evaluation when we could more effectively promote growth in clients by giving them a realistic evaluation. The successful casemanager, in responding appropriately to his or her clients' feelings and problems, demonstrates the capacity to have both a "hard head and a soft heart". In the opinion of the writers, this last point is at the core of professionalism in criminal justice.

THE PSYCHOSOCIAL ASSESSMENT PROCESS

In addition to establishing a therapeutic relationship with his or her parolees or probationers, casemanagers in generalist or in the counselor roles must also understand the study or psychosocial assessment process before working with their clients. This step is sometimes referred to as the diagnostic phase. The psychosocial assessment process forms the basis from which an identification of the problems in social and psychological functioning derive. In addition, the psychosocial assessment process suggests avenues for treatment or intervention in order to move parolees and probationers toward personal rehabilitation and societal reintegration goals. In this section of the Chapter the nine steps that are involved in this process are described. Two points need to be emphasized here. First, it should be noted that in real life such a process is dynamic and on-going since data regarding the probationers and parolees change or are added and, consequently, assessments and treatment approaches are often changed or modified. Second, each step in the process is built upon the previous step and, consequently, the progression is assumed to be linear. Instead, more often than not, the dynamic interaction between the parolee or probationer and the casemanager is uneven and characterized by periods of both acceleration and regression and more commonly resembles a matrix.

The **first step** is the identification of the problem or problems to be solved. The problems that clients in the criminal justice system present are usually multiple in nature. These problems usually center on criminal behaviors or acts by the clients which bring them into contact with the criminal justice system. The presentation of the problem or problems in social functioning begins as the casemanager, via the therapeutic relationship with the client, allows the client to present his or her view of the problem, and of his or her role in its formation. In the case of multiple problems, the casemanager may wish to prioritize these problems and focus on the most pressing ones. In the prioritization process, problems that can be readily addressed with the provision of concrete services, e.g., economic assistance, medical services, educational services, employment services, etc., or problems that can be managed by information and referral services, should be immediately acted-upon at this stage.

The essential goal that has to occur at this step is the development of a therapeutic relationship with the client. Without such a relationship the client may not feel comfortable about entering into a planned change process. At this point it is also important that the client be emotionally or psychologically able to acknowledge that he or she has a problem(s) in social functioning which brought them into contact with the criminal justice system. That is to say, the client has to "own the problem." The client must also be experiencing a certain amount of social and emotional stress in regard to these problems and be motivated to the point of being willing to engage in a planned change process with the casemanager. The caveat for the casemanager here is to clearly understand that in order to bring about some resolution of the problem(s), the parolee or probationer must be willing, in a genuine and authentic way, to admit his or her role in the formation of the problem(s), and be motivated to use the help of the casemanager. If this condition does not hold then the casemanager's activities toward rehabilitation and reintegration of the client may just end up as "rescue fantasies".

Some signs that point to client modifiability include: feelings of depression, anxiety states, various manifestations of psychological and physiological stress, withdrawal, and feelings and expressions of guilt. Parolees or probationers who may not be able to profit from casemanagement activities need to be eliminated at this point in the process. This category would include, for example, overtly psychotic or schizophrenic clients (a category not likely to be placed on electronic monitoring anyway), and persons with certain kinds of developmental disorders or with certain kinds of organic mental disorders which foreclose on their ability to become involved in logical discussion, appropriate communication, and conceptualization.

It is problematic as to whether or not antisocial personality disorders ought to be included. These authors believe that they ought to be included if two key points can be established: that they are able to admit their role in the problem, even if such as admission is only a surface response; and, if they show some sign of remorse or guilt about their behavior. By contrast, if their behavior is more likely characterized by rationalization, projection and displacement of guilt and blame, denial of the behavior, and various kinds of anti-social and asocial ideations and manipulations, they are probably not suited for electronic monitoring. In short, clients who do not have the emotional or psychological capacity and ability to understand and act upon the real world of the "here and now" usually cannot be helped by cognitive-behavioral methods because these are reality-level therapies.

The question becomes, then, what types of parolees or probationers are suitable planned change targets for casemanagers? The types of problematic behaviors presented below are a suggested but not exhaustive list of those most likely to benefit from such intervention:

> 1. Persons with certain kinds of disorders of infancy, childhood, or adolescence, e.g., conduct disorders.
>
> 2. Persons with psychoactive substance-induced or substance-use disorders, for example, alcohol, amphetamine, cannabis, cocaine, hallucinogen, inhalant, opioid, and phencyclidine types.
>
> 3. Persons with certain kinds of sexual disorders, such as, exhibitionism, pedophilia, and voyeurism.
>
> 4. Persons with impulse control disorders, for example, kleptomania, and pyromania.

5. Individuals with certain kinds of personality disorders, e.g., antisocial personality disorder (see previous comment about antisocial personalities), borderline personality disorder, and sadistic personality disorder.

6. Persons with various types of anxiety disorders, but, particularly, people with post-traumatic stress disorders.

7. Persons with problems in personal relationships including interpersonal relationship problems in parental, marriage, and family functioning, and problems in relationship to other siblings, parents, relatives, friends, co-workers, and employers. Symptoms include difficulties in role relationships, communication problems, sexual dysfunctions, problems in parenting skills, and anxiety.

8. Problems of generalized anxiety while in certain environmental situations such as: applying for job, taking a test, being interviewed, writing or presenting a report, meeting new people. Symptoms include phobias, feelings of powerlessness and hopelessness, poor self esteem, learned helplessness, selfdefeating thinking patterns, rationalizations about failure, depression, withdrawal, and self isolation.

9. Problems of educational insufficiency including lack of a high school diploma or G.E.D. certificate, poor skills in written English, poor verbal communication skills, difficulties with understanding the norms of appropriate job and workplace behavior and performance, problems of job stress and time management, poor skills in the use of basic communication devices in the everyday workplace, e.g., telephones, calculators, typewriters; computers.

The **second step** has to do with placing the client's problems in both an historic and present context. The major activity that the casemanager becomes involved in at this point is that of data gathering in terms of the broad socio-psycho-environmental context of the client. The casemanager at this juncture is "looking over the terrain" of the probationer or parolee with respect to the most pressing social problems that were presented in the previous step, while simultaneously gathering data that will result in a better understanding of the client. The point is to develop an ecological perspective about the parolee or probationer. Sources for these data include family members and relatives, friends, co-workers, employers, and all sorts of collaterals that are or have been important in the client's psychological and sociological life space. These sources should also include other agencies and services that the probationer or parolee may have used in the past. From all of these sources the casemanager begins to get an idea of the nature and scope of the probationer or parolee's social problems and some inkling about how to intervene in terms of problem resolution.

During the **third step**, the casemanager hypothesizes about the client's problems in social functioning. This is done as he or she synthesizes the data presented by the client in step one with the data about the client's social and psychological environment obtained during step two. What the casemanager should do here is to speculate about the cause-effect relationships among these data. This step results in a tentative diagnosis or assessment of the problem or problems in social functioning.

At **step four** the casemanager must go about confirming the tentative assessment which had been developed in step three. At this point the casemanager begins to focus his or her thinking about what kinds of additional data are needed and how one would go about obtaining these data in order to accept or reject the tentative assessment. When possible, data obtained from offenders should be corroborated by other sources.

Step number five involves the operationalization of step number four. Here, the casemanager begins an active process of obtaining data with respect to the specific confirmation or denial of the tentative assessment. In contrast to step number two, the focus here is very narrow. This is the point at which the casemanager may examine various reports and documents concerning the client. Now, various types of tests and measurements may be used, such as: health and medical examinations, psychometric tests, educational measure-ments, and work and vocational evaluations, etc. This is also the point at which one may wish to consult with other human service experts such as, psychiatrists, clinical psychologists, clinical social workers, physicians, nurses, and counselors/therapists of various sorts. It may also become necessary to refer the parolee or probationer for additional testing or evaluation if needed. At this step in the process the casemanager is trying to obtain highly focused data concerning the problems of the probationer or parolee in order that he or she can have some degree of confidence concerning the assessment. A kind of "sorting out" concerning the validity of problems in social functioning has to occur here.

At **step six**, the casemanager should have arrived at a point where the data that he or she has obtained strongly suggests that the tentative assessment of the probationer or parolee's problems in social functioning appears to be accurate. Also, the tentative assessment at this point seems to suggest or support a plan of treatment or planned intervention with respect to the modification or remediation of the social problems in order to facilitate the rehabilitation of the offender and to promote his or her reintegration into society. At this point the casemanager should feel confident about formulating his or her plan of action for planned change intervention. If this comfort level has not been achieved then the casemanager needs to continue to gather and evaluate the data base. Particular scrutiny should be directed at the client's view of the problems and at data from collateral sources; especially, data derived from persons that are socio-culturally and emotionally close to the client, i.e., "significant others." A reiteration of steps one to four may be in order.

In **step seven**, the casemanager draws-up a design or strategy for intervention. Such a plan always includes a set of short-term and long-term (more than one year) planned intervention goals, along with a set of actions or techniques, expressed in behavioral terms, to accomplish these goals. These goals and sets of actions are tailored to each of the parolee or probationer's social and psychological problems. The plan must always involve the casemanager and the client in the change process. Intervention plans must recognize the principle that casemanagers intervene with and on behalf of the client. There has to be mutuality, agreement and therapeutic work by both parties. Sometimes it is important to reduce both sets of activities to a written contract or casemanagement grid. This type of procedure helps to strengthen the client's acknowledgment of the problems and foster responsibility for working toward their resolution. [12]

Step number eight is the actual "doing" of the intervention. It is the "putting" into action of the planned change strategy. Implementation of the treatment plan will be discussed in the next part of this Chapter.

The last **step, number nine**, refers to evaluating the planned change efforts. It should be understood that evaluation occurs on an on-going basis as the work continues with the client, i.e., on the basis of incomplete goals. Evaluation also occurs at termination; whether the goals have been achieved or not or are incomplete. In the instance of incomplete goals, the casemanager must constantly monitor the client's progress toward attaining the goals and the effects of the interventions. If progress toward the goals is not being effectuated, or if the goals have not been achieved within the time-frame for the intervention effort, the casemanager must begin a review of the steps in the intervention process. He or she must closely examine the data bases in steps one and two of the process to determine if the data are reliable.

Consideration must also be directed at the assessment to determine if the assessment was accurate. At termination, a final evaluation also must occur with respect to the goals that have not been achieved. Again, the casemanager must look at the data bases in steps one and two as well as his or her assessment of the problems in social function. With respect to goal attainment, examining the data bases and the assessment serves as a kind of "feedback" loop. In areas where the interventions are not or have not been successful, an examination of the data bases serves as a corrective. In the examination new data may become apparent or the data may be viewed in alternate ways. This, in turn, will affect the assessment, and, ultimately, may cause the casemanager to venture into different intervention avenues.

There are a number of quasi-experimental types of clinical outcome models available for the evaluation of individual or group casemanagement goals. The nine steps in the psychosocial assessment process can fit nicely into these types of single-subject, group or multi-group designs.[13] The authors recommend their use when casemanagers desire a more quantitative, i.e., less impressionistic, evaluation of the degree of attainment of the casemanagement goals.

CASEMANAGEMENT PLANNED CHANGE INTERVENTION

Previously in this Chapter, the writers argued in favor of cognitive-behavioral theory as a theoretical base for underpinning casemanagement activities with parolees or probationers on electronic monitoring. In this portion of the Chapter descriptions of casemanagement roles for planned change interventions with these populations will be presented.

Casemanagement Generalist Roles

Casemanagement generalist roles can be thought of as a series of actions or techniques or strategies that the casemanager engages in with and on behalf of the client in order to effect their social and physical environment. The intention is to impact and change or modify the social and physical environment of the client in some sort of "concrete" or direct way. The areas for change, modification or adjustment in the client's life derive from the treatment goals that were established during the psychosocial assessment process. In short, the casemanager generalist is a social diagnostician who functions as a sociotherapist, rather than as a psychotherapist, in order to help the parolee or probationer on electronic monitoring and home confinement achieve his or her treatment goals of rehabilitation and reintegration into society.

Casefinding Role. In this role the casemanager generalist functions as a social epidemiologist. In that sense it is an "outreach" role that encompasses early identification of problems in the social and physical environment that may pose future risks for the client on electronic monitoring. Having identified some of these risk factors, the casemanager generalist must then try to prevent them from impinging upon or altering the course of successful rehabilitation and reintegration. It is a primary casemanagement technique that consists of detection and prevention.

Networking Role. This role is sometimes described in the literature about generalist or casemanagement practice as the "broker" or "linkage" role. In this role the casemanager generalist may apply several strategies on behalf of the probationer or parolee on electronic monitoring in order to facilitate a successful monitoring experience. Networking cannot be successful unless the casemanager   understands the structure and function of the community in which he or she works. The casemanager also has to have a good deal of technical expertise about the various programs and services for which his or her client may be eligible. It is also predicated upon the casemanager having a profile in the community's criminal justice and social services arenas. The casemanager,   therefore, would need to have established a network of professional and collateral contacts that could be utilized in order to secure needed services for the client. Sometimes networking can be conducted at arms-length via a process of information and referral. Many communities now have computerized information and referral services networks. Networking, however, often must transcend the technological and informational levels. A successful casemanager must know the service delivery system not only in terms of its programs and services but also in terms of its   personnel. Networking means utilizing the human personal touch in order to help the client access the social and rehabilitation services systems.   Sometimes it is built upon a reciprocal or quid-pro-quo basis. The key element, however, is the quality and efficiency of the interpersonal-interprofessional network that the casemanager as generalist builds and cultivates.

Advocate Role. Sometimes the casemanager has to act more assertively or aggressively on behalf of parolees or probationers on electronic monitoring in order to help them achieve their reintegration or rehabilitation goals. This occurs when the opportunity structure of social services is blocked, fragmented or incomplete, or does not exist. When these kinds of situations occur in a community the casemanager often must advocate on behalf of his or her client. The advocacy role can be played-out in a number of ways. The casemanager may lobby on behalf of his or her client by virtue of presenting technical or factual data in the client's favor for admission to a program or service. The argument may also be fashioned in a rational-logical mode via a consideration of the advantages and disadvantages of developing a particular program in the community or a special service in a existing agency.   The effort may center on a humanistic consideration of the client and his or her family circumstances when advocating for the admission of the probationer or parolee into a program or for extending the eligibility of certain services to them. Or, an appeal can be directed at various agency directors for coordination of various programs and services, or to individual agency directors concerning the issue of closing gaps in fragmented service areas. The advocate, of course, has to lobby or argue persuasively or, perhaps, confront various audiences. The range of such audiences, in both the public and private sectors, might range across individual program or service providers or executives, community criminal justice advisory groups, social services councils, and various city, municipality, county, or state human services commissions. Obtaining memberships in some of these groups is a secondary gain for the casemanager. Ultimately, what the casemanager generalist as a successful advocate achieves is a humanizing of bureaucracies.

Enabler Role.   In the enabler role the casemanager helps   the client maximize the use of appropriate programs and services in the community. Many types of enabling activities are contained within this role. For example, a basic stance is one of describing and discussing information about various programs or services and the array of associated options, contingencies and opportunity costs associated with each program or service with the client. This is followed by encouraging the client to act on the information. Another stance might involve the expression of a professional opinion concerning the importance or the need for the client to use a certain program or service. This kind of enabling is important for clients who may have certain psychological or developmental deficiencies which make it difficult for them to make responsible or rational choices. Sometimes they need to "float" upon the ego of the casemanager.

The classic enabling activity involves the use of support. This can take the form of verbal reassurances as well as non-verbal supportive clues, such as body language. These activities may be used to convey the message that there may be some hope; that something can be accomplished; that there may be some "light at the end of the tunnel". The use of imagery techniques, for example, could be used at this junction. At the far end of the enabling scale, perhaps a kind of "friendly persuasion" may be in order. This activity may be operationalized via a logical discussion with these individuals concerning the social and personal costs and benefits in relation to using or not using the programs or services.

There are some important considerations in the enabling process that need to be considered.   The enabling process must first be tempered with an understanding by the casemanager that the program or service that he or she is promoting is appropriate for the client and that the client should have a reasonable chance of success in the program.   Second, the casemanager cannot enable clients to act on a goal unless they are willing or motivated to take action. We cannot create motivation. We can, however, promote people toward motivation by support, reassurance, encouragement, and, when appropriate, by persuasion or even threats.   With regard to persuasion, sometimes the process of logical discussion, when directed at the client and his or problematic life situation, may stimulate a measure of anxiety, or perhaps create a crisis mentality which may cause them to become motivated to make use of a service. But we must not use force or coercion unless no alternative is present.   Similarly, we cannot want or wish for them to accomplish something out of our own needs for self-reassurance, ego-gratification or self-aggrandizement. Conversely, the casemanager generalist must respect their right to self determination in terms of acting on service options, even if that self-determination is ultimately exercised in a self-defeating way. Oftentimes success derives from failure.

Casemanagement Counselor Roles

The casemanager as counselor focuses upon the intrinsic aspects of the client, i.e., the personality system, in order to bring about social and behavioral change with respect to the treatment goals. The casemanager as counselor role with probationers or parolees on electronic monitoring is based upon three assumptions that the writers have constructed from cognitive-behavioral theory. These assumptions correlate with the viewpoint of the phenomenolog-ical nature of mankind.

The first assumption is that the individual can create his or her own social reality and, further, that this occurs through conscious processes. The second assumption is that an individual can create his or her psychological reality via conscious processes. The third assumption rests on the point of view that society is a human product. In short, it is the aggregate or the sum of individual creations of social and psychological realities. In holding to this sort of phenomenological view, the casemanager as counselor is, ipso facto, a reality-level therapist. The focus is on "today and now". When working with the parolee or probationer this means that unconscious processes, for example: repressed and suppressed feelings, are not addressed unless they have become   problems of social and psychological living in the "here and now." Similarly, a traumatic developmental history which may have been characterized by abuse and neglect is only addressed if these traumata can be defined as   directly linked to current problems in social or psychological functioning. In practice, the casemanager focuses his or her counseling efforts upon the cognitive, affective and behavioral aspects of the personality structure of the parolee or probationer by utilizing some or most of the roles described below in order to help these persons achieve the rehabilitation and reintegration goals that were established during the psychosocial assessment process.

Modeling Behavior Role. In this role, the casemanager as counselor projects or models for the probationer or parolee stereotypes of normative, i.e., socially and psychologically acceptable attitudes, values and behaviors.   The casemanager, in the course of the therapeutic relationship with the client, demonstrates appropriate ways of dealing with life and its problems and contingencies in keeping with normative attitudes, values, and behaviors. It is an educational or teaching role. Pullias and Young describe the kinds of life problems and experiences that the successful counselor as teacher ought to project to his or her clients:

> The teacher who meets the class has also lived life to this
> point and bears in his personality the wounds and scars of
> that experience. He comes to the teaching responsibility as
> a personality who also has developed a style of life, a way
> of dealing with his needs and the demands of the environ-
> ment. It is hoped that special study and training, growth in
> self-understanding and perhaps in wisdom will have healed
> some of the worst wounds and produced a style of life better
> than that of the less experienced students. (P. 94).[14]

If the process has been effective the client will have incorporated some of the norms and will model or play them out in his or her own life style. It is not possible to measure in any clinical way how the process of incorporation takes place because it is an unconscious process. Furthermore, the behavior or attitude that is being modeled may not be external but may, instead, be internal. The behavior or attitude or value may be composed of elements of a certain kind of look or way of dress or some other kind of positive imagery in the persona of the casemanager with which the client attaches.   The casemanager may not be aware that an incorporation has occurred. Often, however, there are physical or verbal clues. For example, the client might say: "I want to get a college degree too so that I can be a correctional officer like you." Or, the casemanager might notice that over time the parolee may have adapted her style of dress and the use of cosmetics in parallel with the casemanager. Modeling behavior is such a powerful therapeutic device that entire social service agencies in the youth field are designed around this approach, for example, Big Brothers and Big Sisters, Inc.

Discussant Role. In this role, the casemanager as counselor engages the parolee or probationers in a process of discussion during which the client is forced to logically consider:

> 1. His or her role in the formation of the problem.

> 2. The consequences and effects of his or her behaviors and actions both in the individual sense as well as the impact of the behaviors or actions upon other significant individuals and larger personal and social systems with which the client interacts.

> 3. Alternative, i.e., more socially acceptable ways of responding, as well as a consideration of contingencies and opportunity costs associated with various ways of behaving and responding.

The purpose of logical discussion is in keeping with the cognitive-behavioral approach and the idea of the phenomenological nature of mankind. Through logical discussion the casemanager brings to the awareness of the probationer or parolee those areas of individual construction of psychological or social reality that are adverse or in opposition to the aggregate of socially acceptable behaviors or actions. The process, thus, involves a verbal consideration of issues and options for the purpose of client awareness. This is usually followed, in sequence, with the next role which has as its outcome the attainment of insight by the client.

Therapist Role. Almost without exception, psychotherapeutic approaches (and, especially, psychoanalytic, i.e., Freudian and neo-Freudian approaches) are insight-oriented change strategies. Insight-oriented therapies are directed toward giving the client insight or understanding about the genesis of their problematic behaviors or actions. Most differences of opinion about this point center on the role and importance of developmental history and the role of suppressed and repressed psychological material (the unconscious). For Freud, insight meant that we could understand our striving and perhaps control or redirect them in the sense that we did not have to become prisoners of our history but could, instead, act upon various choices. But acting upon choices was voluntary. Adler was more emphatic about this issue.

For Adler, an individual could change the reality of his or her sense of "inferiority" by conscious actions and should be persuaded to act upon various choices by the therapist. Jung, by contrast, equated insight with a kind of universal religious order though which a person could become be "saved". (Pp: 16-26).[15]

The three variations on the theme of insight are presented by way of background so that the casemanager as counselor may understand that insight is a very problematic concept. In actuality, insight may be better understood as a construct. That is, we cannot observe, empirically, that a probationer or parolee has gained insight but we can infer that such a process has occurred via a demonstration of a change in behavior or attitude. For example, the parolee or probationer may have gained insight about the effect of his behavior upon someone else as he or she expresses feelings of guilt about the behavior. From the expression of guilt we infer the attainment of insight. In terms of the casemanager as therapist role, he or she is concerned with the development of insight for the purpose of bringing to the client's awareness the array of choices that he or she may wish to act upon in order to change or modify his or her social and psychological situations and to move or direct them to act on positive choices. To be effective in this role the casemanager must help the client understand his or her problems and must encourage he or she to change problematic behaviors and attitudes. In other words, with this population and in this kind of setting, insight is not enough. Probationers and parolees need to be directed to act upon that insight. Cooperation between the probation officer and the primary counselor is critical to this process.

More specifically, the process of client insight-development flows as an extension of the process of logical discussion discussed in the previous step. Insight develops as the probationer or parolee on electronic monitoring is forced to reflect on or consider:

1. The nature of his or her personality and how this might contribute to problem formulation. For example, the passive-dependent client who "lives" in a psychologically retreatist subculture of drug addiction and prostitution, and whose chronic responses to life's demands are denial and repression, might be forced to consider the usefulness of these kinds of mal-adaptive responses. This could occur as the casemanager forces her to clarify her expressed feelings that "no one like or loves her and that others always take advantage of her". This sort of client might come to understand that her weak self concept creates difficulties for her in life because this imagery of herself "sets-her up" to expect that people will mistreat her, and that this imagery moves her, like an invisible hand, toward addiction and prostitution.

2. His or her behavior or actions and how these may contribute to problem formation. For example, an asocial client might be directed to consider the nature of his aggressive reactions to other people and how these kinds of actions might provoke retaliation. This can evolve via a consideration of a parolee's statement that "people are just no good and you have to get them before they get you". Here, via logical discussion, the client would be directed to reflect upon the usefulness of aggressive responses, a consideration of more appropriate behaviors and actions, as well as an exploration of the maladaptive ego response: the rationalization that the aggression is "ok" because people are going to "get you". With respect to the last point, the client would be forced to consider that the rationalization might be serving to help he or she avoid stress, or self blame, or as a justification for avoiding an unpleasant task.

3. The dynamic of developmental history (especially the impact of experiences of abuse and neglect as a child) as these negative experiences impact   upon current problems in social or psychological functioning.   For example, a probationer who continually makes unwise choices for men in her life and, as a consequence, gets caught-up in criminal activity, would be moved to consider and reflect upon her current state. This might come about as she shares with the casemanager her recollection of physical abuse by her father as a child and his statement to her that she would "never be any good". Insight to help move her toward behavioral change could occur as the casemanager as counselor interprets her behavior in the "here and now" as a kind of self-fulfilling prophecy that is being played-out by her conscious choice of men who abuse her: a choice that springs from unconscious feelings about her father that had been repressed or suppressed.

CASE EXAMPLE

A case example will now be presented in order to illustrate how the cognitive-behavioral approach could be used to structure casemanagement generalist roles and casemanagement counselor roles with probationers or parolees on electronic monitoring. Of course, as previously noted, the process starts with the development of a therapeutic relationship and proceeds to logically flow from the psychosocial diagnostic assessment. Those are the "givens" in this example.

Case Vignette. Ms. A is a white, 44 year old single mother who has a 12 year old son. She completed the tenth grade and has only marginal work skills. She has spent most of her employment life in menial positions. She is a cocaine and heroin user and has been most recently arrested for burglary. She supports her addictions by burglary and   petty theft. Her son has been removed from her care by the child welfare department because of chronic neglect and lack of supervision. He has been placed with a foster care family. Ms. A is very depressed. She is currently on electronically monitored parole.

Casemanagement Generalist Roles with Ms. A

Casefinding Role:

* Identify and clarify the source of her depression by referral to the local county mental health agency, university teaching hospital facility, or state mental hospital.

Networking Role:

* Refer Ms. A. to the local high school's adult education department for enrollment in its G.E.D. program.

Advocate Role:

* As a member of the local human service resource commission for X city, you try to influence the other members of the commission to support the application of Y agency for a "seed" grant from the city in order to develop a narcotics treatment program.

Enabler Role:

* You provide Ms. A with information from the local child welfare protective services agency about the conditions that pertain to visiting her son at the home of his foster parents.

Casemanager Counselor Roles with Ms. A

Modeling Behavior Role:

* You discuss some of the difficulties you experienced in trying to complete your college degree in criminal justice while having to work twenty hours a week. Discuss how you were able to balance out your work and school schedule. Draw a verbal analogy between how you were able to accomplish this and her need to obtain a G.E.D. so that she could progress beyond menial jobs.

Discussant Role:

* Have her describe for you her life as a cocaine and heroin addict. As she draws this picture point out the consequences of her behavior in terms of her arrest and the removal of her son.

* Engage in some futurism exercises with her by verbally painting two scenarios: in one scenario she continues to smoke "crack" and "shoot-up" heroin and eventually becomes so addicted that she has to be institutionalized, or she"overdoses" and dies. Then paint a different scenario in which she enters a treatment center and successfully completes the program and joins Narcotics Anonymous. Following this, she completes her G.E.D. certificate and eventually becomes employed as a computer operator and is reunited with her son. Ask her to describe for you what attitudes, behaviors and actions that she would have to demonstrate in order to play-out the positive life script.

Therapist Role:

* Ask her to describe for you what kind of a person she thinks that she is. In the course of the discussion she tells you that she feels that she is not very pretty, that she is "dumb", and that no one could ever really love her for herself. She tells you that she has always felt this way about herself, even as a child. In the course of the discussion you, as the casemanager, begin to reflect or "bounce" these feelings that she has about herself upon her. You do this by forcing her to consider if there is a link between her poor self concept and why she commits burglaries and petty crimes and has become addicted. A reflective question to her might be: "Could it be possible that because you feel so poorly about yourself you take cocaine in order to escape from yourself and from your problems"? The task here for the casemanager is to allow the client to reflect upon her social and psychological construction of her personality and help to make the link between this definition of herself and her problems in social functioning. This may promote insight-formation as you make her reflect upon her construction of the reality of her personality.

* Ask her to describe for you why the child welfare department removed her son from her care and placed him with a foster family. As she recounts the situation, and as you ask her to elaborate upon various circumstances, it develops that she believes that her need for drugs means that she has to have a "fix" regularly and that while she is "high" she can't always supervise her son. Also, as she describes it, even with a regular job, much of her income has to go to support her drug habit, therefore, she cannot always buy enough food or clothing for him. These things, she explains, plus the lack of support

from the father of the child and her rejection by her family, force her to steal in order to exist. At this point the casemanager forces her to reflect upon her behavior by asking her to consider that her description of the situation involving the reasons for the removal of her child was constructed by her upon a base of rationalizations for behavior: ("I'm an addict, therefore, I have to have do drugs"); denial of her role in the problem formation by taking upon herself the role of the victim; and, projecting the blame upon others, such as her family and the father of the child. Although there may be a realistic base to support some of her arguments, she cannot be allowed to "feast" upon these arguments.   In reality treatment approaches, such as cognitive-behavioral approaches (and especially with criminal justice populations), clients are not allowed to "rationalize away" mal-adaptive behaviors. Instead, she has to be helped by the casemanager to understand the linkage between her distorted ideations and how these serve to construct an inappropriate social and psychological reality: a reality at odds with conventional society. From this process insight may develop and, hopefully, with encouragement of the casemanager, she will act upon that insight.

* The casemanager as therapist asks Ms. A to recount her family history. In that discussion she reveals that she was sexually abused by her step-father beginning at age eight, and that her mother chronically neglected her physical and emotional needs in favor of a younger sibling. At the age of 12 her mother was deserted by her husband and the family became destitute and "went on welfare", i.e., Aid to Families with Dependent Children. One night while mother was visiting her boyfriend, Ms. A's younger sister accidentally set the mattress in the apartment on fire. Shortly thereafter, child protective services caseworkers investigated and she and her sister were temporarily placed in a shelter home. Eventually, they were returned to the custody of the mother. As she tells her story, the casemanager may ask her if she sees any parallels between her past life script and the current way that she is functioning with respect to her son. The parallels are not precisely the same but they are very similar. The casemanager tells her that sometimes when we have been traumatized as children; as adults we tend to play-back the same script with our children.   This   unconscious awareness moves toward conscious awareness as the casemanager causes her to reflect upon this issue in her developmental history.   When she demonstrates an understanding of the link (achieves conscious awareness) between her family history and her current problems in social functioning, insight is formed. The next point, as always, is to help her exercise the option of constructing a more socially and psychologically acceptable social reality. A reality in accord with social norms.

SUMMARY AND CONCLUSIONS

In this Chapter the authors have argued in favor of the use of the cognitive-behavior approach by casemanagers in order to facilitate the personal rehabilitation and social reintegration of parolees and probationers on home confinement via electronic monitoring. The was accomplished by an analysis of the theoretical base of the approach, both historically and currently. In addition, some research support concerning the effectiveness of this method was presented. Two important preconditions for casemanagement were also described in detail: the nature of the therapeutic relationship and the psychosocial assessment process.

Research support from the clinical literature concerning the most important facilitating conditions of effective therapists were identified as well as the important personality characteristics of counselors who functioned in an empathetic manner. The process of casemanagement was discussed and specific descriptions were presented concerning the casemanagement generalist and the casemanager therapist, including a description of roles and a presentation of examples.

Increasingly, clinical outcome research with clients in mental health settings seems to suggest that cognitive-behavioral approaches hold the promise of being effective treatment strategies. There is some data to suggest that it may be a useful method for working with persons in the criminal justice system; particularly, with delinquent youth. By extension, the authors conclude that this may also be true of other special populations within the criminal justice system such as probationers and parolees on electronic monitoring. In the future, this assertion will be tested given the explosive growth of electronic monitoring programs now in evidence in this country across city, county, state and federal criminal justice jurisdictions. The authors believe that such a test may well demonstrate the efficiency and effectiveness of this approach.

NOTES

1.   Robert E. Kennedy. Cognitive Behavioral Interventions with Delinquents, in Andrew Meyers and W. Edward Craighead (eds.), Cognitive Behavior Therapy with Children (New York: Plenum Press, 1984), pp. 351-376; Anthony A. Hains and Ann Higgins Hains, Cognitive-Behavioral Training of Problem-Solving and Impulse Control with Delinquent Adolescents, Journal of Offender Services and Rehabilitation Vol. 12 (1988), pp. 95-113.

2.   Dieter Weiss. Psychoanalytic Schools from the Beginning to the Present (New York: Jason Aronson, 1973).

3.   Harold D. Werner. Cognitive theory, in Francis J. Turner, (ed.), Social Work Treatment: Interlocking Theoretical Approaches - 3rd ed. (New York: Free-Press, 1986), pp. 91-130.

4.   Arnold A. Lazarus. Introduction and Overview, in Arnold A. Lazarus, (ed.), Multimodal Behavior Therapy (New York: Springer Publishing Company, 1976), pp. 4-8.

5.   Charles B. Truax and Kevin M. Mitchell. Research on Certain Therapist Interpersonal Skills in Relation to Process and Outcome, in A.A. Bergin and S.L. Garfield, (eds.), Handbook of Psychotherapy and Behavior Change: An Empirical Analysis (New York: John Wiley and Sons, 1971), pp. 299-344.

6.   Carl R. Rogers. Client-Centered Therapy (Boston: Houghton Mifflin Company, 1951).

7.   Dean H. Hepworth and JoAnn Larsen. Direct Social Work Practice, 2nd ed. (Chicago: The Dorsey Press, 1986).

8.   Thomas Keefe and Donald E. Maypole. Relationships in Social Service Practice (Monterey, CA: Brooks/Cole Publishing Company, 1983).

9.   Betty D. Meador and Carl R. Rogers. Client-Centered Therapy, in Raymond Corsini, (ed.), Current Psychotherapies (Itasca, IL: F.E. Peacock Publishers, Inc, 1974), pp. 119-165.

10.   Felix Biestek. The Casework Relationship (Chicago: Loyola University Press, 1957).

11.   Carl R. Rogers. The Necessary and Sufficient Conditions of Therapeutic Personality Change, Journal of Consulting Psychology, Vol. 21 (1957), pp. 95-103.

12.   Richard Enos and Mary Hisanaga. Goal Setting with Pregnant Teenagers, Child Welfare, Vol. 58 (1978), pp. 541-552.

13.   Srinika Jayaratne and Rona L. Levy. Empirical Clinical Practice (New York: Columbia University Press, 1979).

14.   Earl V. Pullias and James D. Young. A Teacher is Many Things (Bloomington, IN: Indiana University Press, 1969).

15.   Philip Rieff. Introduction, in Philip Rieff (ed.), Freud-The History of the Psychoanalytic Movement (New York: Collier Books, 1963), pp. 16-23.

CHAPTER 6

DESCRIPTIONS OF THE USE OF ELECTRONIC MONITORING IN
THREE SELECTED PROBATION DEPARTMENTS AND REPORTS OF
STAFF SATISFACTION WITH THE TECHNOLOGY

INTRODUCTION

The purpose of this Chapter is to provide the reader with detailed descriptions
about some of the electronic monitoring programs in current use. Toward this
end, the authors have obtained data from three large metropolitan probation
and parole departments: The Dallas County (Texas) Adult Probation
Department[1]; the Harris County (Houston, Texas) Adult Probation Department[2]; and, the Harris County (Houston, Texas) Parole Office.[3] These
departments were chosen because of their size, the diversity of their client
caseloads, and because of their use of "state-of-the-art" electronic monitoring
technologies. In addition, this Chapter contains the results of a survey
research effort directed at discerning the attitudes and levels of satisfaction of
the criminal justice staff members in these three departments with respect to
the use of EM in their departments.

DALLAS COUNTY ADULT PROBATION DEPARTMENT

At the time of this study, Dallas County had a population of 1,833,100. The
city of Dallas is the largest city contained within the county. The total
population in the county included 419,852 males over 25 years of age. Of
these, 72.6% had a high school diploma and 61,351 held college degrees. The
county was 71.4% white, 17.6% black, 9.5% Hispanic, 1.1% Asian and 0.4%
American Indian. Only 16.3% of Dallas County's population was classified as
rural by the U.S. Bureau of the Census.[4] The county had a 5.7% unemployment rate. In 1985, 183,712 serious crimes were reported to police and 17,322
(9.4%) of these crimes involved violence.[5]

The Dallas County Adult Probation Department exercises a control-strategy
probationary method. This approach emphasizes supervision and restitution
rather than personal adjustment and rehabilitation. The department deals with
clientele in a major urban center and many of its probationers reside in the
inner city. Client socioeconomic statuses range from lower-class to middle
class. The majority of the clients served by this department are Hispanic or

black, work at relatively low-paying jobs or were unemployed at the time of this study.[6]

The Dallas County Adult Probation Department offers both group and individual counseling, in addition to referring clients to Alcoholics Anonymous, Narcotics Anonymous, Al-Anon, etc. The department encourages the use of community resources which include: substance abuse and chemical dependency programs; elder assistance programs; child care programs; educational programs; emergency assistance programs; employment assistance programs; halfway houses/emergency services; health needs; immigration services; legal aid services; mental health/mental retardation agencies; mental health practitioners; veteran's services; vocational and physical rehabilitation services; and, women's concerns programs. The Dallas Department also makes use of the Community Control Program (CCP) which was developed to provide the courts with a sentencing option.[7] This program has two goals: (1) to decrease the growth of the prison population and associated costs and (2) to satisfy, at least in part, the demand that criminals be punished. This program provides increased surveillance and services to probationers who have failed to comply with traditional probation programs. This program uses electronic monitoring to assist the surveillance effort.

The purpose of the CCP is to provide an alternative to prison while continuing to protect the community through surveillance and control of the offenders by utilizing appropriate resources. The offender is confined to his/her residence where strict non-institutional sanctions are imposed. To facilitate this, the CCP provides a constant, around-the-clock surveillance through electronic monitoring. This program uses a team approach and restricts their caseload to 25 cases per team.

An offender is eligible for CCP if the courts order it; if the offender is subject to a hearing on a "motion-to-revoke"; or if the offender is a "shock probationer". The offender must also meet the following criteria:

1. The probationer should request CCP.

2. The probationer should have "something to lose" if he/she absconds.

3. Probationers must have a telephone in their home and have a RJIIX connecting jack.

4. The probationer must have been convicted of a felony.

Two CCP officers are assigned to a caseload of 25 probationers. One officer acts as the surveillance officer and the other officer is a casework officer. The surveillance officer's primary responsibility is to provide surveillance services, such as: home and job visits, drug and alcohol screening, and to maintain regular contacts with the EM agency. The casework officer assists the surveillance officer and provides casework services, including: job placement, planning activities in conjunction with other court ordered programs, and also maintains each case file. The casework officer must also write a "supervision summary report" at the end of the first 45 days in the program and after three months in the program in relation to each probationer's progress. This report focuses on areas such as personal, legal, home, and employment problems, as well as attitude and adjustment issues.

The CCP Team is responsible for the following at the initial visit of the probationer:

1. Issue and review the CCP Handbook (which describes the program) with the probationer.

2. Explain any "special conditions" with the probationer.

3. Explain CCP's expectations of the probationer.

4. Notify the EM agency and arrange for the hook-up.

5. Briefly explain the EM system to the probationer.

6. Prepare a "daily activity log" with the probationer's schedule.

7. Discuss consequences of violations.

8. Review the monthly report.

9. Have the probationer report immediately to his/her home for the EM hook-up.

10. Go to the probationer's home with the monitoring representative to hook-up the system.

The CCP officers must complete training in "Computerized Cases Classification", "Strategies for Case Supervision" (SCS), and "Case Planning/Document-ation". The reasons for placement in CCP must be submitted and justified for each CCP probationer accepted into the program. An intake form must also be completed so that it is easy to identify a probationer. The purpose of SCS is to provide a more efficient and effective case management system. An assessment is made to aid the officer in making decisions on the risks and needs of the offender. Information is gathered from the pre-sentence investigation report, by reviewing relevant reports, by interviewing the family of the probationer, by interviewing the victims, and by interviewing the probationer. A supervision plan is then completed for each CCP probationer in order to assure close attention to the problems and needs of the offender. The same information gathered at intake is also gathered at the discharge level in order to evaluate the effectiveness of the program.

Each probationer will have a minimum of three face-to-face contacts with the officer per week. There will be at least two face-to-face field contacts each week and at least four face-to- face contacts on the weekends during the month. The probationer must report weekly to the casework officer. Those who are unemployed must report daily, Monday through Friday. The CCP team will make at least two contacts with collaterals, including: employers, family members, and others who are in a position to facilitate the supervision objectives.

If a probationer is placed on CCP, he/she must adhere to certain special conditions of probation. Some of these conditions are as follows:

1. The probationer must reside at a specified address.

2. The probationer must observe approved hours of absences.

3. The probationer is responsible for the financial costs of EM services.

While a probationer is on CCP status, he/she is under house arrest. The offender is restricted to the residence with the only exceptions being employment, court-ordered activities, and life-threatening emergencies. All CCP probationers will be expected to maintain employment and work schedules are submitted to the officer weekly. The probationer must provide CCP officers with proof of employment. Those who are unemployed will be allowed time to search for work, but these search efforts must be carefully documented and given to the officer weekly. The court-ordered programs must be approved in advance and noted on the "Daily Activity Log" weekly. In the event of a life-threatening situation, the offender must try to contact the officer first, if he/she is unable to reach the officer then he/she must provide the officer with written verification within 24 hours.

Two types of EM devices are used in Dallas County. One is a continuous signaling device that consists of a transmitter attached to the probationer's ankle with a receiver installed in the home. The probationer is to remain within a 150 foot radius of the receiver or the host computer will indicate an absence. The system operates 24 hours a day, seven days a week. This system is used to indicate whether or not the offender is at home. The other type of system is the Luma Video Phone System. In this system, the Luma Video phone is placed in the probationer's home. The EM agency makes random calls to the home and asks the probationer to send a photo through the Luma system to verify his/her presence in the home. With both systems, the agency will notify the probationer's surveillance or casework officer in the event of a violation of house arrest.

There are two categories of violations, minor and major. Minor violations are discrepancies (absences) of 30 minutes or less. In these cases, the officer is not immediately notified. Major violations are discrepancies of 31 minutes or more. In these instances the officer is notified immediately; i.e., no later than the following business day. When the officer is notified, he/she will try to confirm the violation. If there is a violation the CCP Staff will contact the court of jurisdiction. After the EM probationer successfully completes the CCP, he/she will be transferred to an Intensive Service (ISP) caseload or to a Specialized Supervision Caseload (SSC). This transfer must be ordered by the court. Any changes in the duration of EM must be agreed upon and ordered by the court.

Many benefits seem to be inherent in the CCP. For instance, it costs less than jail or prison; the offender remains in the community with a job, thus supporting him/herself and, paying taxes. Many probationers pay part, if not all, of their own monitoring fees. In addition, the CCP helps to reduce the overcrowding of jails and prisons. Those offenders with communicable diseases will have reduced the cost of isolation and medical care that a jail or prison is required to pay. Furthermore, the CCP will also help avoid the damaging experience of a young offender going to jail or prison.

As of August 18, 1989, 75 probationers on CCP were being monitored. This number changes daily because probationers will either complete the program, abscond, be revoked, or commit a new offense and be in jail. The department has the capacity to handle 120 EM clients. In the month of December 1989, 23 offenders were hooked-up to the system. In January 1989 approximately

44 were hooked- up. In February, approximately 63 were hooked-up. And, in March, approximately 77 were hooked-up.

In interviews with Dallas County Adult Probation Department staff, several staff members indicated that the main problem with EM was that the equipment sometimes registered false violations. Specifically, because of technical problems with the equipment, the devices were recording violations of offenders leaving their residences when, in fact, they had not left. They also mentioned other minor problems, such as the clients complaining about "cabin fever," being "watched" 24 hours a day, and being awakened at odd hours of the night as a result of random phone verifications.[6]

HARRIS COUNTY ADULT PROBATION DEPARTMENT

During the time of this study, Harris County had a population of 2,604,882. This figure included 661,038 males over 25 years of age; and, 72.0% of those had a high school diploma while 98,302 held college degrees. Houston is the largest city within Harris County. The county was 65.6% white, 18.1% black, 14.1% Hispanic, 1.9% Asian and 0.3% American Indian. Only 13.4% of Harris County's population is classified as rural by the U.S. Bureau of the Census.[4] The County had a 10.3% unemployment rate. In 1985, 213,322 serious crimes were reported to police and, 20,462 (9.6%) of these crimes involved violence.[5] Like Dallas County, the majority of the Harris County probationary clients were from lower and middle socioeconomic classes. Occupations ranged from managerial types of employment to the chronically unemployed. The Harris County Adult Probation Department, just as the Dallas County Probation Department, utilizes EM through a contractual arrangement with a private vendor, Program Monitor, Inc. (PMI). The capacity of their EM program is 90 with an average caseload of 25-30 clients per officer.[2]

The Harris County Adult Probation Department utilizes EM to monitor regular and ISP offenders in their special programs division. Electronic monitoring is employed as a diversion from incarceration in jail in order to help reduce jail overcrowding. Their program has four criterion for placing offenders on EM:

1. The offender must have committed a felony offense.

2. The offender must be in custody at the time of placement.

3. The offender must have a telephone at time of placement.

4. The offender must remain on EM for 90 days.

In addition to the criteria described above, clients' eligibility for the program are conditioned upon:

1. A demonstration by the probationer of a lack of stability and self-discipline.

2. Evidence that the probationer has a social history containing unplanned and spontaneous acts with negative results.

3. Indications that probationers who are chemical abusers are being monitored thus restricting further opportunities for repeated chemical abuse.

4. Data that probationers who are convicted of sex offenses will need intensified supervision of their movement in the community.

5. Evidence that probationers with a history of violent or assaultive behavior are being monitored for the safety of the community.

Clients on EM are required to turn-in a schedule each week indicating the times when they were out of their residences. Legitimate client absences from a residence include: work, church, medical treatment, shopping, and court appointments. All other client out-of-residence activities must be presented in writing and approved by the probation officer. Clients must report to the probation office twice monthly and allow visits to their home once a month. Any reported violation is investigated the same day. Clients must follow all of the other stipulations of probation imposed, as well as those imposed as a result of being placed on EM.[8]

HARRIS COUNTY PAROLE OFFICE

A control-strategy is also utilized by the Harris County and Parole Office.[3] Control-strategy emphasizes supervision and restitution. The office also utilizes other ancillary programs, such as: Alcoholics Anonymous, Narcotics

Anonymous, and Project Rio, a local offender re-integration program, to help facilitate its efforts of supervision and restitution.[9]

In Harris County parole officer caseloads are specialized along several dimensions. Clients on EM constitute one such group of specialized caseloads. Six parole officers and one supervisor routinely supervise these offenders. Supervisors in the Harris County Parole Office assign only parole officers who have experience and have expressed interest in EM to a specialized EM caseload.

Other specialized caseloads located in the board (e.g. sex offenders, drug offenders) occasionally employ electronic monitoring with some of their more problematic clients. The services in the specialized caseloads for sex offenders emphasizes rehabilitation over supervision. The sex offenders in this caseload are closely monitored and are required to have psychiatric treatment and/or mental health services, counseling, and various types of individual and group testing.

The Harris County Parole Office has established the following parole releasee eligibility criteria for placement on EM:

> 1. The releasee must chronically fail to adjust to the requirements of the specialized caseload to which they are assigned.

> 2. The releasee must fit the following set of circumstances

>> a. The releasee was convicted of DWI where there was evidence of continuous alcohol abuse.

>> b. The releasee was convicted of non-assaultive crimes and was unemployed for thirty days after completing Project Rio.

>> c. The releasee missed more than two consecutive appointments with their case-load officer.

>> d. Be a releasee who has pending charges and has been released on bond or had current warrants against them withdrawn.

    e. A releasee who refuses to submit to urinalysis, or who submits two positive samples.

    f. A releasee who was placed on EM in lieu of a summons.

    g. A releasee who refuses needed treatment.

The Harris County Parole Office requires a minimum of four face-to-face (offender-parole officer) contacts per month. Releasees are placed on one of two levels for the purpose of EM feedback from EM contractors. On level one, the officer is required to visit the offender if the reason for a EM signal interruption is not resolved by telephone. At level two, violations are reported the following day. Releasees are moved from level two to level one if there are two EM interruptions in the signal during one month. The releasee's progress in the program essentially determines the level at which he/she is dealt with during his/her time in the program.

Electronic monitored offender case conferences are held with a supervisor if a releasee fails to attend two scheduled counseling sessions in one month, fails to return home at a scheduled time, or leaves home at unapproved times on three or more occasions for more than thirty minutes. If the offender is continuously violating the conditions, an officer can request that additional special conditions be imposed, such as: letters of reprimand and case conferences with the supervisor; referral to specialized treatment; referral to quarterhouse; summons hearing; referral to Bexar (San Antonio, Texas) County Parole Violator Facility; or a pre-revocation warrant request. A releasee is terminated from EM by: either successfully completing the program by remaining on minimal supervision status for four months, or by being revoked for any cause.

The Harris County Parole Office is also involved in a Pre-Parole Transfer Program (hereafter referred to as PPT). This program also uses EM. The PPT program is designed to place inmates in residences in the community in order to offer a humane, real-life situation that provides opportunities for self-improvement. The goal of this program is to assist inmates in developing good working attitudes, habits, and marketable skills as well as a lifestyle necessary to reintegrate successfully into society.

The operation of the PPT program requires coordination between community services, parole staff, the Texas State Department of Corrections (TDC), and the EM service provider or vendor. Community services staff of the TDC at Huntsville, Texas, screen all cases for EM eligibility, and the community resource officer at the PPT facility interviews and approves or disapproves the selection of inmates for admission into the program. The community service staff at Huntsville also contacts Program Monitor, Inc., and arranges for the inmate to be attached to the EM devices prior to his/her release. The emphasis of the PPT/EM program is on control and reintegration primarily because the clients are still considered to be in the custody of the TDC. His/her freedom is restricted to verified employment, verified job search or job readiness programs, and other absences approved in advance by the PPT/EM officer. The PPT/EM officer makes six face-to-face visits each month with every inmate, and makes a visit a week to their residences.

If PMI reports a violation, the officer must, within one hour, attempt to verify the escape. If the officer cannot reach the inmate by telephone, then he/she must call local law enforcement authorities in order to make arrangements for them to accompany the officer to the residence. The officer must make visual verification of the inmate's absence. If the client is not there, the officer must notify the TDC of an escape.

The inmates in the PPT program must complete 30 days of intensive counseling and orientation in an approved community correctional facility prior to transfer. If the inmate is eligible for release to a halfway house, the officer must then provide a security package which consists of 3" x 5" photograph of the inmate; the inmate's correspondence and visiting list; his/her record summary; a record of the inmate's prior residences and employment; and any other pertinent information in the inmate's file.

When screening private residences certain conditions are followed. The residence must comply with certain specific criteria which include:

> 1. A stable family of some duration; no ex-offenders in the residence.
>
> 2. Liquor not sold or distributed on the premises.
>
> 3. Illegal drugs not known to have been consumed, sold, or possessed on the premises.
>
> 4. Other illegal activities are not know to have occurred in the residence.
>
> 5. No adverse family situations present.

6. Adequate transportation available, and/or telephone communication is easily accessible.

The PPT/EM officer is required to visit the inmate six times per month; once a week at the residence, and also make contacts with the client's employer when necessary.

A progress report is conducted after 30 days of supervision and 30 days prior to the inmate's parole date. If an inmate tries to escape, the officer: verifies the facts of the escape; notifies the administrator of the PPT by phone; files a complaint with the local justice of the peace; obtains a warrant; delivers it to the local law enforcement office; and, advises the administrator of the warrant number, issuing authority, precinct number and county. If an inmate is arrested locally, the officer contacts the administrator, completes an incident report and delivers the report to the inmate 24 hours prior to the hearing. A hearing is conducted unless waived by the inmate.

PROBATION AND PAROLE OFFICERS' SATISFACTION WITH ELECTRONIC MONITORING: QUANTITATIVE RESEARCH DATA

For this study,[10] the authors developed a "private vendor satisfaction survey questionnaire" in order to examine probation and parole officer satisfaction with EM in general and with EM as provided to their department by a private vendor previously discussed, PMI. A sample of 30 probation and parole officers completed the questionnaire. All of these officers were working with electronically monitored offenders in either Dallas or Harris counties.

The survey instrument consisted of a 25-item questionnaire which included forced choice questions concerning the effectiveness of EM, PMI, the equipment, as well as open-ended items that solicited specific suggestions in re to improving the system. The majority of the respondents were parole officers (80%). Fifty-seven percent of the parole officers were from Dallas County and 23% were from Harris County. The remaining 20% of the respondents were probation officers from both counties. Sixty-seven percent of the probation officers were from Dallas County and 33% were from Harris County.

Questions 1 and 2 were directed at determining how the officers rated EM in comparison to regular probation/parole and intensive supervision. More than two-thirds (66.7%) of the total sample of officers rated EM as more effective than regular probation/parole, while the remaining 33.3% of them rated it as less effective or about as effective as regular probation/parole.

Approximately seventy-two (72.4%) of the officers also rated EM as more effective than intensive supervision, whereas the remaining 27.6% of the officers felt it was less effective or about as effective as intensive supervision. Thus, probation/parole officers seem to view the effectiveness of EM as approximately the same for both regular probationers/parolees and intensively supervised offenders (72.4% and 66.7% respectively).

The total sample of officers was subsequently divided into several different types of groups in order to further analyze the responses to Questions 1 and 2, as well as to enhance the scientific quality of the survey. These analyses sought to determine if any significant differences existed in the ratings by officers across agencies and regions. A t-test was used to measure the statistical significance of differences between the mean responses. No significant difference was found to exist between the parole officers located in Dallas and Harris counties regarding their ratings of the effectiveness of EM versus regular parole ($T=1.2$; $P=0.24$) or intensive supervision ($T=0.80;P=0.43$). However, the extremely small size of the samples of Dallas and Harris county probation officers makes the use of this particular type of statistical analysis problematic. Therefore, any inferences that are drawn from these data should be considered as preliminary. However, visual inspection of the data suggest a similar distribution of responses among probation officers.

By subdividing the total sample into two other groupings: (1) probation officers; and, (2) parole officers, and again employing a t-test for statistical significance, no significant statistical difference was found to exist at the .05 level between probation officers and parole officers concerning their ratings regarding the question of whether or not EM was more or less effective than intensive supervision ($T=1.90$; $P=.068$). However, probation officers were found to more often rate EM as more effective than regular community supervision than were parole officers ($T=3.14$; $P=.004$). One possible explanation for this significant difference in attitudes may be related to the fact that restricted confinement (confinement to their residences as part of EM) is novel to probationers in general. It may, therefore, produce a more apparent impact on this population than it does on parolees who have experienced confinement in prison prior to confinement as part of EM.

Questions 3 through 6 inquired about the impact of EM on the probation/parole officers' performance of their job roles. Of the total sample of officers completing the questionnaire, 80.0% stated that EM made their jobs harder. Two specific reasons for this were offered by respondents: (1) EM increases the number of revocations, resulting in more "paperwork" for them; and, (2) the logistical demands of EM require officers to spend more time in direct contact with clients. More than fifty-six percent (56.7%) of the officers stated that, due to EM, there was less time to conduct other duties, while the other 43.3% indicated that EM resulted in about the same amount of time or an increase in the amount of time available for other duties.

Questions 7 and 8 addressed the benefits of EM for offenders and their families. The majority of the officers sampled (76.7%), indicated that EM was beneficial to their clients. However, only 30% of them felt that EM was beneficial to the families of EM clients. Interpretations of these beliefs are difficult to make, but it seems reasonable to suggest that officers fear that offenders will vent the frustrations produced by home confinement and behave more aggressively at home.

Questions 9 through 12 dealt with the monitoring equipment itself. Of all the officers in the sample, 23.4% had clients who had experience with both continuous and random EM systems. One-third (33.3%) of the officers had clients who had only been on continuous monitoring, and 43.3% had clients whose exposure was solely to random monitoring. Over forty-six percent (46.7%) of the officers indicated that the equipment was dependable, however, the majority (53.3%), claimed that the equipment was unreliable. Two of the specific problems identified by the officers who had indicated that the equipment was unreliable were: (1)   ankle straps broke, causing the equipment to cease working; and, (2)   any accidental tampering with the equipment caused interference with the telephone, which in turn caused violations to be reported when no violations had in fact occurred. As far as equipment maintenance was concerned, 53.3% indicated that the equipment was adequately maintained, while 46.7% thought the equipment was poorly maintained.

Questions 13 through 16 queried the attentiveness of PMI to the needs of officers and their clients. Their views of PMI's attentiveness to their needs were virtually identical with their views of PMI's attentiveness to the needs of their clients. Half of the officers in the sample thought PMI was attentive to their needs as well as to the needs of their clients, while the other half of the sample disagreed, claiming that PMI was inattentive to both their needs and to those of their clients. Suggestions made by those officers who felt PMI was inattentive to their needs included: (1)   more follow-ups on equipment repairs and hook-ups; (2)   more attention to the computer printouts with regard to violations; and, (3)   more attention to the accuracy of violation reports. Suggestions made by those officers who viewed PMI as inattentive to the needs of their clients included: (1) pay more attention to which type of EM system (continuous or random) the client is assigned; (2)   reduce unnecessary telephone calls to randomly monitor clients; and, (3) be neither inconsiderate nor overly cordial to officers and clients.

Questions 17 through 19 were directed at ascertaining the information provided to the officers by PMI about the clients. Of those surveyed 63.3% claimed PMI provided most of the information needed by them, while 36.7% claimed they did not. More than seventy percent (74.1%) indicated that the neglected information was important, whereas 25.9% viewed this information as relatively unimportant.

Questions 20 and 21 dealt with PMI's ability to promptly connect and disconnect clients to EM equipment when requested. More than fifty-six percent (56.7%) indicated that PMI usually honored their requests in a timely fashion, while the remaining 43.3% felt they did not. The time delays in hooking-up clients to the EM equipment after PMI received the request varied from 4 to 8 days in most cases.

The last four questions in the survey, Questions 22 through 25, solicited overall ratings of PMI and the electronic monitoring program. Of all the officers in the sample, 56.7% claimed that overall PMI provided poor or extremely poor service, while the remainder (43.3%) disagreed and claimed that PMI provided adequate to extremely good service. Again, the total sample of officers was subsequently divided into several different types of groups in order to further analyze the results concerning the officers ratings of PMI's service. This was done to determine if any significant differences existed in the ratings by officers from within and across agencies regarding these ratings, and to strengthen the inferences that one might draw from the study. One grouping consisted of the four geographical locations. The t-test results indicated a significant difference at the 0.05 level of significance between the parole officers located in Dallas and Harris counties regarding their ratings of PMI' service ($t=2.0$; $p=0.05$). Dallas County parole officers were found to have rated PMI's services higher than did Harris County parole officers. Here again, the extremely small sample size of the Dallas and Harris county probation officers places restrictions upon the nature and type of generalizations that one can draw from the analysis of these data.

The sample was next subdivided to test for differences between probation and parole officers. The results of the t-test indicated no statistically significant difference between probation officers and parole officers concerning their ratings of PMI's service ($t=0.00; p=1.00$).

When asked what they would prefer to have their department/office do concerning the provision of EM services, 13.3% indicated that they would prefer to have PMI continue to provide EM services under the current arrangements, another 13.3% indicated that they would prefer to continue having PMI provide EM services, but would modify the contractual arrangement with PMI, 30.0% indicated that they would prefer switching to another private vendor for the provision of EM services, and the remaining 43.3% indicated that they would prefer to have their own department/office directly provide this service.

The last question (Question 25) inquired as to whether officers would prefer to continue utilizing EM. Approximately forty three percent (43.3%) indicated that they would strongly insist that EM be continued; 20.0% indicated that they would insist that EM be continued; 26.7% indicated that they had no preference regarding continuing EM or doing away with it; 6.7% indicated that they would insist on getting rid of EM; and the remaining 3.3% indicated that they would strongly insist on getting rid of EM. Thus, at least for this sample, EM appears to be fairly popular among probation/parole officers despite the perceived increase in workload and the logistical problems encountered with the contractor.

SUMMARY AND CONCLUSIONS

This chapter contains original material derived from a study conducted by the authors to measure the effect of private sector electronically monitored home confinement on adult probationers and parolees and the levels of staff satisfaction with EM.[10] Descriptions of EM programs are included from: The Dallas County (Texas) Adult Probation Department; the Harris County (Texas) Adult Probation Department; and, the Harris County (Texas) Board of Pardons and Paroles. This Chapter also contains specific descriptions of the types of clients served by these three programs, details concerning the eligibility criteria for enrollment in the programs, and specifics concerning the operation and technical details of these programs. Quantitative data regarding satisfaction with EM provided by a private vendor was derived from a study of the staff at the Dallas County Adult Probation Department and from the staff at the Harris County Adult Probation Department.

The Dallas County Adult Probation Department exercises a control-strategy probationary method. This approach emphasizes supervision and restitution rather than personal adjustment and rehabilitation. This department does, however, offer both group and individual counseling and makes use of client referrals to various social service treatment agencies for remediation of certain problems experienced by the offenders assigned to their department. This department also uses the Community Control Program which is an option for diversion from incarceration. Electronic monitoring is employed in conjunction with this program.

In Harris County EM is used as a diversion from jail in order to reduce jail overcrowding. The Harris County Parole Office also uses a control-strategy. In both of the Houston programs the emphasis is, again, on supervision and restitution. As with Dallas County, both Houston departments make a great deal of use of client referrals to social services treatment programs; especially, substance abuse programs.

In addition, the State Board of Pardons and Paroles emphasizes special caseload programs structured along the lines of types of offenders, i.e., sex offenders, drug offenders, offenders with communicable diseases. In these programs, rehabilitation is emphasized. Electronic monitoring is sometimes used with these populations and, especially, with their more difficult clients.

In conclusion, across the departments studied, the writers noted that one of the most important findings was that most of the probation and parole officers seemed to view the effectiveness of EM as approximately the same for both regular probationers/parolees and for intensively supervised offenders. And, furthermore, that a majority of these officers (43.3%) wanted to continue the use of EM in their departments while only 6.7% wanted its use discontinued.

In the opinion of the writers, continued research studies, such as the one conducted by the writers, need to be implemented so that a database base may be developed that over time will allow for scientific inferences to be drawn concerning the use and effectiveness of this new and important technology in the criminal justice field.

NOTES

1.   Dallas County Adult Probation Department. Dallas County Community Services (Dallas, TX: Dallas County Adult Probation Department, 1989).

2.   Harris County Adult Probation Department. Personal Communication, 1989.

3.   Harris County Board of Pardons and Paroles. Specialized Caseload Procedural Manual (Houston, TX: Harris County Board of Pardons and Paroles, 1989).

4.   U. S. Department of Commerce.   General Social and Economic Characteristics (Washington, DC: U.S. Department of Commerce, 1983).

5.   U. S. Department of Commerce.   City and County Data Book (Washington, DC: U.S. Department of Commerce, 1988).

6.   Dallas County Adult Probation Department. Personal communication, 1989.

7.   Dallas County Adult Probation Department.   Community Control Program Operations Manual (Dallas, TX: Dallas County Adult Probation Department, 1987).

8.   S. L. Patton.   Jail Diversion - An Electronic Monitoring Program (Houston, TX: Harris County Adult Probation Department, 1988).

9.   Harris County Board of Pardons and Paroles. Personal communication, 1989.

10.   John E. Holman, James F. Quinn, Clifford M. Black, and Richard Enos. A Study of the Effects of Private Sector Electronically Monitored Home Confinement on Adult Probationers and Parolees (Denton, TX: University of North Texas, Institute of Criminal Justice, 1990.)

CHAPTER 7

A STUDY OF THE EFFECTS OF ELECTRONICALLY MONITORED HOME CONFINEMENT ON OFFENDERS AND THEIR HOME ENVIRONMENTS: METHODOLOGY, INSTRUMENTATION, AND DEMOGRAPHY

INTRODUCTION

Chapters 7 and 8 contain a description of a study which was conducted by the writers in order to evaluate the effects of electronically monitored (EM) home confinement on felony offenders and their family environments (members and significant others). This Chapter deals specifically with the research methodology, the survey instruments used in the study to gather the data, and describes, in detail, the socio-demographic and criminologic characteristics of the parolees and probationers who were the subjects of the study. The study was funded by the Criminal Justice Division of the Office of the Governor of the State of Texas [#SF-89-602-2394].

Electronic monitoring of offenders is essentially so new that it is still in its infancy and literally has no history. The technology is at present experiencing continual growth and development. This is particularly true with respect to the increased computerization of the systems. With something as new as EM, it is perhaps unrealistic at this time to expect the organizations experimenting with the development and implementation of EM in criminal justice settings to be at little more than rudimentary stages of development of the technology. That is to say, the intra-organizational and inter-organizational relationships of the agencies involved in the use of EM have until now faced a plethora of new and unknown problems. These sorts of contingencies are likely to color the immediate future of EM. The analogy that seems most appropriate here is that of EM to open heart by-pass surgery. When open heart by-pass surgery first appeared it was developed and implemented by a few physicians who were confronting the unknown. Today, open heart by-pass surgery is viewed as somewhat common-place. In essence, EM is at the very beginning of its development and many problems continue to present themselves for resolution to the pioneers who are using it as a form of intermediate sanctioning.

Pioneers, such as Program Monitor, Inc., need to be recognized for their role in its development. This is not to say that such pioneers and the organizations that they represent should be exempt from criticism. Instead, such criticism needs to be placed in a proper context. Evaluators must remain salient of the fact that the work of pioneer organizations in the field created the base from which others can build. Thus, it is the hope of the writers that the readers of this Chapter and the Chapter that follows will view the results of our study, and our interpretations of the data derived from the study, in the spirit in which they are offered, i.e., as an attempt to enhance our knowledge of EM, and which, in turn, should benefit all criminal justice professionals involved with the technology. As with any innovation, errors of judgment, especially in the area of relative priorities, are both inevitable and instructive. Indeed, these errors contribute to both our comprehension of this new area of criminal justice practice and to the sort of development by which innovations eventually become standardized methods.

METHODOLOGY

Several different methodological approaches were used in this study. One approach consisted of the psychometric testing of EM probationers and parolees, and the collection of socio-demographic information directly from EM probationers and parolees themselves. A second approach was to collect information directly from significant others living with offenders on EM. A third approach utilized the collection of information directly obtained through the use of a questionnaire from probation departments, parole offices, and the private EM vendor involved with EM in the jurisdictions included in this study. A fourth approach employed interviewing probation and parolee department staff. A fifth, and final approach, consisted of observations made on behalf of the researchers involved in this study. Although each of the methodological approaches used in this study will be discussed separately in the sections that follow, a real strength of employing multiple methods of observations, i.e., triangulation, is that it allows for an empirical synthesis of various observations on a single phenomenon.[1]

All subjects included in this study were adults on probation or parole for felony offenses who resided in either Dallas, Denton, or Harris counties within Texas. Participation was voluntary with a signed consent form allowing information to be used in the final report on the study and for publication. All of the data used in this study was collected in calendar year 1989, with the exception of the pretests conducted in Denton County which were collected in December of 1988. While the primary interest of the researchers was on the effects of EM on these offenders, the study also employed control groups of probationers and parolees who were not on EM. The use of such control groups allowed for a four-group, pretest/posttest, pre-experimental, research design to be conducted.[2] The four groups used in this approach were: (1) EM probationers; (2) EM parolees; (3) non-EM probationers; and (4) non-EM parolees.

Dallas and Harris counties were chosen for their relatively large population of EM offenders, and Denton County, also located in Texas, for the inclusion of some non-urban offenders. The researchers met with representatives of each of the agencies involved in the study to introduce the instruments being used and establish a logistical format for the administration of these instruments.

Pretest and posttest procedures were identical within individual probation departments and parole offices, however, they were different across departments and offices. Probationers were examined at the local offices to which they were required to report on a monthly basis. The research was conducted on normal reporting days for all probationers included in the study.

Probationers were administered the instruments at the various probation offices by the research staff conducting this study, whereas parolees were administered the same devices at their residences by their parole officers. While this difference in test administration procedures is problematic in that the stimuli associated with the study's instrumentation varies according to whether the subject was on probation or parole, it also provided several advantages. Group testing of probationers was time-efficient and the coordination of testing with routine reporting at the probation office resulted in minimal inconvenience to subjects. The joint effect of this approach was to maximize the number of completed instruments.

The administration of these study instruments by parole officers was an innovation on the original study design requested by their respective departments. Parolees did not regularly report to any central location as did probationers. Because of their more serious crimes and/or more extensive criminal histories, as well as their recent release from incarceration, parolees tend to live in the least desirable areas of the cities under study and are generally less receptive to socio-scientific examination than are probationers. This seemed to be the best method of obtaining the data in order to assure researcher safety as well as to maximize the number of completed responses.

Logistics required that parolees be administered the research devices by their respective parole officers during routine visits to their homes. This strategy allowed for a much larger number of offenders to be involved in the study thus drastically reducing the cost of administering the testing devices to parolees. The parole officers involved were, of course, first instructed in the proper administration of the instruments and the intent of the study. Similar procedures were followed in both parole offices despite some minor discrepancies in their internal organizational structure.

The method of data collection for parolees also necessitated modifying the Family Environment Scales (FES) questionnaires for use with this sub-sample of parolees. The 90 statement FES was reduced to two FES subscales (18 true/false questions in order to gather data on the conflict and control dimensions of the instrument). The Beck Depression Inventory (BDI) was not altered in any way.

The initial goal of the study was to test a total of 200 offenders and their significant others residing in their households (co-residents). This goal was surpassed in that data were collected on 261 offenders. The initial goal was modified to include the control groups which greatly strengthens the study, and to reduce the significant others in the study, which to a lesser extent, weakens the study. The addition of the control groups is somewhat self-evident in that they allow for comparisons to be made that otherwise could not be made. The modification of the initial goal regarding offenders' significant others residing in their households had to be made essentially for two reasons: (1) the relatively large number of offenders living alone, thus the absence of a significant other to be involved in the study; and (2) the logistics of administering testing devices to significant others. Very early in the study attempts were made, but subsequently discontinued, to either have the significant others accompany their respective probationer or parolee when they reported, or to return self-administered testing devices with the probationers or parolees, or to return them by mail.

ASSESSMENT INSTRUMENTS

The main testing instruments used were the Beck Depression Inventory and the Family Environment Scale. By employing the BDI and FES, the use of EM was evaluated to determine if the program was successful in facilitating offender mental health status and integration (in the case of probation) or reintegration (in the case of parole) into a law-abiding family and community.

A pretest/posttest design was used with an intervening period of approximately two and one-half months for each subject. The elapsed time period chosen between pretests and posttests was based on the recommendations of the technical staff of the electronic monitoring vendor, Program Monitor, Inc.(PMI), who stated that the average time per offender on EM was approximately three months.

SOCIO-DEMOGRAPHIC QUESTIONNAIRE

Each offender completed a Client Demographic Information Form, which was kept in his/her confidential file, and was assigned an identification number. This form was used to identify and collect the following information: (1) the name of the offender; (2) the agency having jurisdiction over the offender; (3) the county having jurisdiction; (4) the specific type of supervision program; (5) general offender socio-demographic characteristics; and, (6) abbreviated criminal histories of the offenders. This form was also used to record test scores and any violations which may have occurred while on the monitoring program.

BECK DEPRESSION INVENTORY

The psychological assessment instrument used was the Beck Depression Inventory. Depression is manifested in many ways and is defined on a continuum from mild transitory effects of feeling low to a severe psychotic depressive state. The BDI was used here to specifically measure dysphoria, as a symptom of depression, rather than depression as a nosologic disorder per se.[3,4,5] It is estimated that the prevalence of psychological disorders is much higher for correctional populations than it is for the general population. For example, Harper and Barry[6] suggest that psychological disorders may involve as many as one-half of all male prisoners.

Various correctional populations (i.e., probationers, prisoners, and parolees) are subjected to major psychological stresses and transitions.[7] Many of the stressors that correctional populations are exposed to have been related to the severity of depression, as well as to the severity of various forms of psychopathology. Thus, the utilization of psychological assessment devices, such as the BDI, for identifying dysphoria among correctional populations, such as those included in this study, is an important part of assessing the effect of the correctional setting, in this case EM, on the offender as a component of the correctional rehabilitative process.[8]

Reynolds and Gould[9] employed both the standard and abridged BDI in their study of individuals involved in a methadone maintenance drug rehabilitation program and found both versions of the instrument to be reliable and valid measures for the assessment of depression. In another rehabilitation setting, Scott, Hannum, and Ghrist[8] employed the abridged BDI in their assessment of depression among newly admitted inmates to a women's reformatory, and reported it to be also reliable as a brief reactive depression screening instrument.

The BDI was developed as a method for identifying and measuring depression.[10] However, it is recommended that the BDI not be used for nosological classification of depression without the collaboration of structured clinical interviews.[5] Thus, the BDI is a 21 item test which reflects physiological, cognitive, and motivational manifestations of depressive symptomatology such as dysphoria.[11] It requires the subject to choose from a set of numbered statements as to how he/she is feeling at the moment. The recommended BDI range of scores 0 to 9 was used to identify normal (non-dysphoric) subjects, and subjects with scores of 10 and above were viewed as suffering from one or more of the levels of dysphoria.[5]

The BDI was chosen as the test instrument because the BDI is among the most frequently used instruments for assessing depression in psychiatrically diagnosed patients[12] and for detecting depression in normal populations.[13] Despite the uncomplicated nature of the BDI questionnaire, the BDI compares favorably with other well-researched instruments measuring depression, such as the Hamilton Psychiatric Rating Scale for Depression, Zung Self-reported Depression Scale, MMPI Depression Scale, and the Multiple Affect Adjective Checklist Depression Scale. Studies have also indicated that the BDI demographic correlates of sex, age, and education for adults is equivocal. However, the relationship of the BDI to race indicates that blacks tend to score higher than whites.[14]

The BDI is relatively simple to administer. Scoring is based on an additive scale ranging from zero to sixty-three (0-63). This is used as a general indicator of the degree of dysphoria experienced by the subject. This instrument is not so precisely calibrated as to divide subjects into homogeneous groups. Rather, BDI scores are a continuous variable and cut-off points are somewhat arbitrary though nonetheless useful in grouping and interpreting data.[3] Traditionally, BDI results are categorized in the following manner:

Score	Interpretation
0 - 9	Normal Range
10 - 15	Mild Dysphoria
16 - 19	Mild-Moderate Dysphoria
20 - 29	Moderate-Severe Dysphoria
30 - 63	Severe Dysphoria

FAMILY ENVIRONMENT SCALE

The Family Environment Scale (FES) measures perceptions of the conjugal or nuclear family, and was used in this study to assess whether the family environments improved, worsened, or remained the same as a result of EM. The FES is a test consisting of 90 true or false statements relating to the subject's perception of his/her family.[15] It is used to assess the subjects' perceptions of their familial environment and is equally applicable to offenders and their family members. Data was organized to allow comparisons of offenders' perceptions with those of their spouses as well as to measure changes in both over time.

The FES is a relatively simple test and can be administered and scored with minimal instruction. The test is divided into three dimensions which are measured by ten sub-scales. The first dimension, Relationship, is measured by the cohesiveness, expressiveness, and conflict scales. The next dimension of Personal Growth (goal orientation) is measured by the independence, achievement orientation, intellectual-cultural orientation, active-recreational orientation, and moral-religious emphasis scales. The third and last dimension on the FES is System Maintenance. This item is measured in terms of the organization and control scales. Each of these areas, when scored, presents an indication of the perceived family environment based on the clients' answers to the true/false statements.

The 90 items for the FES were originally determined from an early version administered to over one thousand individuals in 285 families, representing church groups, high school parent groups, black and Mexican groups, as well as a disturbed clinical group.[16] Normative data were collected from 1,125 representative families and 500 distressed families. Distressed families were contacted through a family clinic, and probation and parole departments. Additional subjects were from families of alcohol abusers, psychiatric patients, and families with troubled adolescents. Other psychometric criteria for selection of items were: an overall true/false response rate for each item close to 50-50, items correlated more highly with their own sub-scales than with any other, and each of the sub-scales had an approximately equal number of items that scored true and that scored false.[17] The final distributions of six of the sub-scales are close to a 50-50 split (mean ranges around 5.5). Only the mean for conflict is low at 3.3. The internal consistency measures for the ten sub-scales range from .61 to .78. The eight-week test-retest reliability coefficients ranged from .68 to .86, and twelve month stabilities ranged from .52 to .89. After controlling for socioeconomic factors, age, and education, distressed families were found to score lower on cohesion, expressiveness, independence, and intellectual and recreational orientation, and higher on conflict and control than the "normal" families in these samples.[18]

There is extensive support for the construct validity of the FES sub-scales. Many other inventories, tests, and assessments of the family environment support the validity of the FES sub-scales. Moos[18] found that religious participation is related to the FES sub-scale of moral-religious emphasis (average $r = 0.62$ for an alcoholic and a community sample); family activities are related to the FES sub-scale of recreational orientation ($r = 0.39$); and family arguments are related to the FES sub-scale of conflict ($r = 0.49$). Moos[19] also reported that families with extensive social network resources scored higher on the FES sub-scales of intellectual/cultural and active/recreational orientation. Assessments of psychiatric outpatients' home environments by professional staff correlated significantly with the individual family member's reports of cohesion, expressiveness, conflict, and religious emphasis.[20]

Druckman,[21] in predicting attrition from treatment programs, found that families who completed treatment had higher pretest scores on the intellectual/cultural FES sub-scale. This could indicated that these individuals are more self-reflective, and at the same time, are more aware of the external world.   Druckman   also found that recidivist families were extremely cohesive. He felt that this may be a dysfunctional factor in these families.[21]

Numerous studies have showed significant changes in pretest/posttest scores for individuals who have gone through crisis intervention and treatment. For example: A group of families was assessed using the FES before, immediately after, and two months after an intensive family therapy program. Significantly increased scores were recorded for cohesion, expressiveness, and independence immediately after the workshop, and additional increases in scores were recorded after two months. A matched, untreated group showed no score change on the FES sub-scales.[22]   Garrison and Weber[23] and Campbell[24] reported reduced family conflict after these families completed a crisis intervention program. The literature is abundant with individual interventions that have led to changes in the family environment as assessed and measured through the FES sub-scales.

DESCRIPTION OF THE SUBJECTS BY GEOGRAPHICAL JURISDICTION

Demographic Description of the Dallas County Probationers

Pretests for Dallas County probationers were conducted in the months of December 1988, January 1989 and the beginning of February 1989. A total of 48 probationers completed the pretests. Posttesting began in March of 1989 with the majority of the tests completed in May. A few were completed as late as October, 1989. Of the probationers involved in this study, three were taken off probation, seven were revoked, two absconded, two were in jail, and one was in a drug treatment facility before or during posttesting. The rest of the probationers completed the posttests, a total of 33.

There were 27 EM probationers in Dallas County that participated in this study. The majority of these offenders (59.3%) ranged from 22 to 35 years of age, and there were more white offenders (63%) than nonwhite offenders (37%). Male offenders were overrepresented with 85.2%. The majority of these offenders were single (55.6%) and had at least 12 years of education (44.5%). The offenses of the offenders on EM ranged from substance abuse crimes, which was the highest (59.3%), to property crimes (22.2%), to violent crimes (14.8%), to crimes against a person (3.7%). Most of the offenders on EM stated that they lived with 3 or 4 people (29.6% each). The majority of the offenders lived with two adults (55.6%) and/or four+ children (51.9%). Most of these offenders (63%) reported having good family relationships.

Concerning drug and/or alcohol abuse prior to arrest, 22.2% indicated no abuse, 7.4% social drinking, 22.2% social use of drugs, and only 3.7% social use of both alcohol and drugs. Of those claiming alcohol and/or drugs as serious problems, 3.7% claimed alcohol, 29.6% claimed drugs, and 11.2% reported both as serious problems. The majority of the probationers claimed that their current alcohol and/or drug abuse usage patterns had drastically changed. By way of illustration, 92.6% reported that they are abstaining from both alcohol and drugs.

Most of this group of probationers had full time employment (59.3%) and worked at unskilled jobs (40%). Of the offenders who were married, the majority of their spouses were unemployed (84.6%). The spouses who did work held jobs that were unskilled (25%) or semiskilled (37.5%).

There were 21 non-EM probationers in Dallas County that participated in this study. The majority of these offenders (47.6%) ranged from 22 to 35 years of age, and there were more nonwhite offenders (52.4%) than white offenders (47.6%). Male offenders were over represented with 71.4%. The majority of these offenders were single (71.4%) and had some college education (38.1%). The offenses of the offenders ranged from property crimes, which was the highest (47.6%), to substance abuse crimes (28.6%), to crimes against a person (14.3%), to violent crimes (9.5%). Most of the offenders stated that they lived with 4 people (28.6). The majority of the offenders lived with two adults (42.9%) and/or four+ children (57.1%). Most of these offenders (61.9%) stated that they had good relationships with their families.

Regarding drug and/or alcohol abuse prior to arrest, 42.8% indicated no abuse, 4.8% social drinking, and 14.3% social use of drugs. Of those claiming alcohol and/or drugs as serious problems, 19% claimed alcohol, 14.3% claimed drugs, and 4.8% reported both as serious problems in their lives. For the majority of the probationers their current alcohol and/or drug abuse usage patterns had drastically changed. Approximately 95.2% reported that they were abstaining from both alcohol and drugs.

Most of this group of probationers had full time employment (66.7%) and worked at semiskilled jobs (31.2%). Of the married offenders, the majority had spouses who were unemployed. The spouses who did work held jobs that were of a clerical nature (50%).

Demographic Description of the Denton County Probationers

The initial Denton County Adult Probation Department posttests began approximately two months after the first pretests were conducted there. Posttests were ultimately completed on twenty-six (26) of the thirty-one offenders. Two significant others were given a pretest. All posttests were completed by March, 1989, except for one of the offenders and his significant other who were retested at a later date due to an illness that required hospitalization. The researchers were unable to obtain posttest scores on five subjects because: three offenders had been taken off probation before posttesting began, one was transferred to the Dallas Adult Probation Department, and the final probationer could not be located.

There were 30 non-EM probationers in Denton County who participated in this study. The majority of these offenders (46.7%) ranged from 22 to 35 years of age, and there were more white offenders (93.3%) than nonwhite offenders (6.7%). Male offenders were over represented at 83.3%. The majority of these offenders were single (56.7%) and had at least 12 years of education (43.4%). The offenses of the offenders ranged from property crimes, which was the highest (40%), to substance abuse crimes (36.7%), to violent crimes (13.3%), to crimes against a person (10%). Most of the offenders stated that they lived with four people (33.3%). The majority of the offenders lived with two adults (43.3%) and/or four+ children (56.7%). Most of these offenders (43.3%) stated that they had good relationships with their families.

In reference to drug and/or alcohol abuse prior to arrest, 17.2% indicated no abuse, 7% social drinking, 13.8% social use of drugs, and only 3.4% social use of both alcohol and drugs. Of those claiming alcohol and/or drugs as serious problems, 10.3% claimed alcohol, 27.6% claimed drugs, and 20.7% reported both as serious problems. For the majority of the probationers their current alcohol and/or drug abuse usage patterns had drastically changed. Finally, 96.6% reported that they were abstaining from both alcohol and drugs.

Most of this group of probationers had full time employment (53.3%) and worked at unskilled jobs (52%). Of the offenders who were married, the majority of their spouses were unemployed (75%). The spouses who did work held jobs that were unskilled (80%).

Demographic Description of the Harris County Probationers

Pretesting of Harris County probationers took place during the end of January, the beginning of February, and in the beginning of April of 1989. A total of 67 probationers took the pretest. The majority of the posttests were completed in April of 1989 with the last posttest finished in October of 1989. Of those probationers who completed the pretest, 48 completed the posttest. A total of nineteen posttests were unable to be obtained for various reasons, including: one probationer was taken off probation before posttesting began; two probationers were at a restitution center; one was placed on regular probation and transferred to another office; two offenders absconded; four were in jail, and three had their probation revoked at the time of posttesting. One of the probationers only finished half of the test. The researchers were unable to locate the last five probationers.

There were 66 EM probationers in Harris County that participated in this study. The majority of these offenders (53%) ranged from 22 to 35 years of age, and there were more nonwhite offenders (56.1%) than white offenders (43.9%). Male offenders were over represented with 81.2%. The majority of these offenders were single (56%) and had at least 12 years of education (43.9%). The offenses of the offenders on EM ranged from substance abuse crimes, which was the highest (53%), to property crimes (36.4%), to violent crimes (6.1%), to crimes against a person (4.5%). Most of the offenders on EM stated that they lived with three people (24.6%). The majority of the offenders lived with two adults (53%) and/or four+ children (51.5%). Most of these offenders (47%) stated that they had   good relationships with their families.

In so far as drug and/or alcohol abuse prior to arrest is concerned, 37.9% indicated no abuse, 9.1% social drinking, 12.1% social use of drugs, and 13.6% social use of both alcohol and drugs. Of those claiming alcohol and/or drugs as serious problems, 7.6% claimed alcohol, 7.6% claimed drugs, and 12.1% reported both as serious problems. For the majority of the probationers their current alcohol and/or drug abuse usage patterns have drastically changed. Also, 91% reported that they were abstaining from both alcohol and drugs.

Most of this group of probationers had full time employment (53%) and worked at manual jobs (27.5%). Of the offenders who were married, the majority of their spouses were unemployed (78.9%). The spouses who did work held jobs that were clerical in nature (28.6%).

Demographic Description of the Dallas County Parolees

Subjects for this study were selected exclusively from the EM specialized unit of this office. In addition to the parole officers administering the study instruments to clients on EM, they were also responsible for administering the study instruments to other parolees who had not been recommended for EM, and who subsequently made up one of the control groups used in this study. Those who were not placed on EM were usually those who refused to participate or who lived with a non-offender who refused to allow the monitoring equipment to be set up in their homes. This control group is thus wholly equivalent to the treatment group except for their (or their family's) attitudes toward EM.

The pretests (a total of 73) were administered during the month of April, 1989. The posttesting began in August of 1989 with only 21 parolees completing the test. A total of 19 parolees were unavailable for posttesting because three were in jail, one refused to take the test, five absconded, four were discharged, six were sent back to the penitentiary. In addition, there were 33 parolees that the researchers were unable to locate.

There were 35 EM parolees in Dallas County that participated in this study. The majority of these offenders (68.6%) ranged from 22 to 35 years of age, and there were more nonwhite offenders (65.7%) than white offenders (34.3%). Male offenders were over represented with 91.4%. The majority of these offenders were single (48.6%) and had less than 12 years of education

(60%). The offenses of the offenders on EM ranged from property crimes, which was the highest (54.2%), to substance abuse crimes (29.2%), to violent crimes (16.6%). Most of the offenders on EM stated that they lived with 3 or 5 people (23.5% each). The majority of the offenders lived with one adult (34.3%) and/or four+ children (42.9%). Most of these offenders (44.1%) also stated that they had good relationships with their families.

Concerning drug and/or alcohol abuse prior to arrest, 29.4% indicated no abuse, and 47.1% claimed social use of both alcohol and drugs. Of those claiming alcohol and/or drugs as serious problems, 23.5% reported both as serious problems. For the majority of the parolees their current alcohol and/or drug abuse usage patterns have drastically changed. In addition, 57.2% reported that they were abstaining from both alcohol and drugs, while 37.1% indicated the social use of both.

Most of this group of parolees had full time employment (45.7%) and worked at manual jobs (40%). Of the offenders who were married, the majority of their spouses were unemployed (77.8%). The spouses who did work held clerical jobs (75%). There were 38 non-EM parolees in Dallas County that participated in this study. The majority of these offenders (55.3%) ranged in age from 22 to 35 years. There were more nonwhite offenders (81.6%) than white offenders (18.4%). Male offenders were over represented with 89.5%. The majority of these offenders were single (73.7%) and had less than 12 years or at least 12 years of education (47.7% each). The offenses of the offenders ranged from property crimes, which was the highest (65.5%) factor noted, to substance abuse crimes (17.3%), to violent crimes (10.3%), to crimes against a person (6.9%). Most of the offenders stated that they lived with six people (22.2%). The majority of the offenders lived with one or two adults (31.6% each) and/or four+ children (50%). Most of these offenders (48.6%) also described their relationships with their families as being good.

In terms of drug and/or alcohol abuse prior to arrest, 32.4% indicated no abuse, and 40.5% social use of both alcohol and drugs. Of those claiming alcohol and/or drugs as serious problems, 27% reported both as serious problems. For the majority of the parolees their current alcohol and/or drug abuse usage patterns have drastically changed. Also, 76.3% reported that they were abstaining from both alcohol and drugs.

Most of this group of parolees were unemployed (64.9%) and those who did work held unskilled or semi-skilled jobs (33.3% each). Of the offenders who were married, the majority of their spouses were unemployed (80%). The spouses who did work held jobs that were clerical (100%).

Demographic Description of the Harris County Parolees

The subjects from Harris County Parole were selected for exactly the same reasons as Dallas Parolees were selected. They were selected from the same types of groups and the officers also administered the tests as did the Dallas County Parole Officers.

Harris County Parolees were given the pretests during the months of April, May, and June of 1989. Pretests were administered to 42 parolees. Of these parolees, 21 completed the posttests which began during the months of October and November of 1989. Some of the parolees were unavailable for various reasons, for example: three were sent back to the penitentiary; one absconded; and one had his parole revoked before posttesting began. The researchers were unable to locate 16 of the parolees.   There were 35 EM parolees in Harris County that participated in this study. The majority of these offenders (71.4%) ranged in age from 22 to 35 years. There were more white offenders (51.4%) than nonwhite offenders (48.6%). Male offenders were over represented at 88.6%. The majority of these offenders were single (51.4%) and had less than 12 years of education (74.2%). The offenses of the offenders on EM ranged from substance abuse crimes to property crimes, which were the highest (48.4% each), to violent crimes (3.2%). Most of the offenders on EM stated that they lived with 3 to 5 people (20.6% each). The majority of the offenders lived with one adult (37.2%) and/or four + children (48.6%). Most of these offenders (62.9%) also stated that they enjoyed good relationships with their families.

Regarding drug and/or alcohol abuse prior to arrest, 21.2% indicated no abuse, 21.2% social drinking, and 36.4% social use of both alcohol and drugs. Of those claiming alcohol and/or drugs as serious problems, 12.1% claimed alcohol, and 9.1% reported both as serious problems. For the majority of the parolees their current alcohol and/or drug abuse usage patterns have drastically changed. Furthermore, 85.7% reported that they were abstaining from both alcohol and drugs.

Most of this group of parolees had full time employment (52.9%) and worked at semi-skilled jobs (27.4%). Of the offenders who were married, the majority of their spouses were unemployed (93.7%). The spouses who did work held jobs that were of an administrative type (33.3%).

There were seven non-EM parolees in Harris County that participated in this study. The majority of these offenders (85.7%) ranged in age from 22 to 35 years. There were more nonwhite offenders (85.7%) than white offenders (14.3%). Male offenders were overrepresented with 100%. The majority of these offenders were single (85.7%) and had less than 12 years of education (71.4%). The offenses of the offenders ranged from property crimes, which was the highest (66.7%), to substance abuse crimes (33.3%). Most of the offenders stated that they lived with three people (42.9%). The majority of the offenders lived with one adult (42.8%) and/or one or four+ children (42.9% each). Most of these offenders (71.4%) stated that they had good relationships with their families.

In terms of drug and/or alcohol abuse prior to arrest, 66.6% indicated no abuse. Of those who indicated alcohol and/or drugs as serious problems, 16.7% claimed alcohol, and 16.7% reported both as serious problems. For the majority of the parolees their current alcohol and/or drug abuse usage patterns have drastically changed. And, 71.4% reported that they are abstaining from both alcohol and drugs, while 28.6% claimed to continue to drink alcohol socially.

Most of this group of parolees had full time employment (57.1%) and worked at unskilled or semi-skilled jobs (33.3% each). Of the offenders who were married, the majority of their spouses were unemployed (100%).

The next Chapter of this book contains the logical extension of the study which comprises the statistical analyses and presentation of the findings. This Chapter then concludes with a section which summarizes and draws conclusions about the entire study.

NOTES

1.   Norman K. Denzin.   The Research Act   (Englewood Cliffs, NJ: Prentice-Hall, 1989).

2.   Donald Campbell and Julian Stanley.   Experimental and Quasi-Experimental Designs for Research   (Boston, MA: Houghton-Mifflin Co., 1963).

3.   Aaron T. Beck.   Depression   (Philadelphia, PA: University of Pennsylvania Press, 1967).

4.   H. J. Lehmann. Psychiatric Concepts of Depression: Nomenclature and Classification,   Canadian Psychiatric Association Journal Supplement, 4, (1959), S1-S-12.

5.   Philip C. Kendall, S. D. Hollon, Aaron T. Beck, C. L. Hammen, and E. Ingram. Issues and Recommendations Regarding Use of the Beck Depression Inventory,   Cognitive Therapy and Research, Vol. 11, No. 3, (1987), pp. 289-299.

6.   D. Harper and D. Barry. Estimated Prevalence of Psychiatric Disorder in a Prison Population,   Abstracts in Criminology and Penology, Vol. 19, (1979), pp. 237-242.

7.   M. Masuda, D. L. Cutler, L. Hein, and T. H. Holmes. Life Events and Prisoners,   Archives of General Psychiatry, Vol. 35, (1978), pp. 197-203.

8.   N. A. Scott, T. E. Hannum, and S. L. Ghrist. Assessment of Depression among Incarcerated Females,   Journal of Personality Assessment, Vol. 46, (1982), pp. 372-379.

9.   W. M. Reynolds and J. W. Gould. A Psychometric Investigation of the Standard and Short Form Beck Depression Inventory, Journal of Consulting and Clinical Psychology, Vol. 49, No. 2, (1981), pp. 306-307.

10.   Aaron T. Beck, C. H. Ward, M. Mendelson, J. E. Mock and J. K. Erbaugh. An Inventory for Measuring Depression, Archives of General Psychiatry, Vol. 4, (1961), pp. 561-571.

11.   J. S. Tanaka and G. L. Huba.   Confirmatory Hierarchical Factor Analyses of Psychological Distress Measures, Journal of Personality and Social Psychology, Vol. 46, No. 3, (1984), pp. 621-635.

12.   C. Piotrowski, D. Sherry and J. W. Keller. Psychodiagnostic Test Usage: A Survey of the Society for Personality Assessment, Journal of Personality Assessment, Vol. 49, (1985), pp. 115-119.

13.   R. A. Steer, Aaron T. Beck and B. Garrison. Applications of the Beck Depression Inventory. In S. Sartorious and T. A. Ban (eds.) Assessment of Depression (Geneva, Switzerland: The World Health Organization, 1986).

14.   Aaron T. Beck, R. A. Steer and M. G. Garbin. Psychometric Properties of the Beck Depression Inventory: Twenty-Five Years of Evaluation, Clinical Psychology Review, Vol. 8, (1988), pp. 77-100.

15.   Moos, Rudolf and Moos, B. Family Environment Scale Manual (2nd ed.) (Palo Alto, CA: Consulting Psychologists Press, 1986).

16.   P. H. Dreyer. The Eighth Mental Measurement Yearbook, (Vol.I) (Highland Park, NJ: The Gryphon Press, 1978).

17.   N. M. Lambert. The Ninth Mental Measurement Yearbook (Lincoln, NB: The University of Nebraska Press, 1985).

18.   Rudolf Moos. Family Environment Scale Manual: A Users Guide (2nd ed.) (Palo Alto, CA: Consulting Psychologists   Press, 1986).

19.   Rudolf Moos. Evaluating Social Resources in Community and Health Care Contexts, In P. Karoly (ed.), Measurement Strategies in Health Psychology, pp. 433-459. (NY: John Wiley Co., 1985).

20.   D. Spiegel T. Wissler.   Perceptions of Family Environments among Psychiatric Patients and their Wives, Family Process, Vol. 22, (1983), pp. 537-547.

21.   J. Druckman. A Family Oriented Policy and Treatment Program for Juvenile Status Offenders, Journal of Marriage and the Family, Vol. 41, (1979), pp. 627-636.

22.   E. Bader. Redecisions in Family Therapy: A Study Change in an Intensive Family Therapy Workshop, Transactional Analysis Journal, Vol. 12, (1982), pp. 27-38.

23.   C. Garrison and J. Weber. Family Crisis Intervention Using Multiple Impact Therapy, Social Casework, Vol. 62, (1981), pp. 585-593.

24.   P. G. Campbell. Sreit Family Workshops: Creating Change in a Family Environment, Journal of Drug Education, Vol. 13, (1983), pp. 223-227.

CHAPTER 8

AN ANALYSIS OF THE DATA CONCERNING THE EFFECTS OF ELECTRONICALLY MONITORED HOME CONFINEMENT ON OFFENDERS AND THEIR HOME ENVIRONMENTS

INTRODUCTION

Analysis of the data proceeds through three basic stages. First, the entire sample is described in terms of sex, age, education, household size, county of residence, and type of program (i.e. parole or probation). This description consists of means, standard deviations, ranges, and frequency distributions and provides a source of baseline data to which sub-groups may be subsequently compared.

The sample is divided into four sub-groups along two basic dimensions - parolees are separated from probationers and offenders on electronic monitoring will be distinguished from controls on ordinary community supervision. This scheme results in four principal subgroups which form an ordinal scale of supervision levels: (1) probationers on regular community supervision; (2) probationers on electronic monitoring; (3) parolees on regular community supervision; and, (4) parolees on electronic monitoring. These sub-groups can and are later collapsed into EM and non-EM groups. The traits of significant others of the probationers are also introduced and compared with those of the parolees. Oneway ANOVA and Scheffe's procedure are used to determine the statistical significance of any differences between groups that are noted in this phase of the analysis.

The four sub-groups of the sample, along with the significant others of the parolees, are described as distinct entities in order to specify a priori differences between these groups that may effect the outcome of inferential tests. This descriptive phase of the analysis is, in part, designed to aid in identifying programmatic distinctions within the sample that are relevant to the interpretation of other findings.

Each of the distinct sub-samples are described and compared with the others on these demographic and criminal history variables. Further description focuses on the client populations of particular agencies within the counties studied. Anomalous distributions are identified at this point in the analysis and the characteristics of the sub-samples are compared.

In the second principal phase of analysis, attention turns to comparisons of the four sub-samples. ANOVA is used to determine if significant differences exist between sub-groups on sex, age, type of offense, employment status, occupational level, education and marital status. These findings facilitate maximum comprehension of the distinctions between these sub-groups on pretest scores.

ANOVA is then used to determine if the family environment of electronically monitored offenders differs significantly from that of controls within the probation and parole sub-groups. ANOVA is then employed to identify the most significant distinctions in levels of dysphoria and perceptions of family environment between the four sub-groups. Regression is then used to specify the most efficient predictors of BDI and FES pretest results within EM and non-EM sub-groups.

In the third phase, attention is focused on the posttest results of the study and their determinants. Beck Depression Inventory and FES posttest results are described for both the entire sample and for each of its sub-groups. The difference between pretest and posttest for the BDI and FES scores are computed for each subject and used as the crucial dependent variable in this portion of the analysis. This analysis will employ the same independent variables as its immediate predecessor but the dependent variable will be the magnitude of individual change on the FES and BDI inventories.

Finally, an additional area was analyzed: The impact of EM on the significant others of the offenders in the study. This additional set of analytical data helped to broaden the inferential picture of the offenders on EM.

DATA COLLECTION

The general problems associated with the collection of original data, such as the collection of data for this study, goes without saying. The data were collected on a voluntary basis on the part of the subjects. There was a heavy reliance on the individual agencies involved to not only make arrangements with the subjects for the data to be collected from them, but also in many instances for these agencies to collect the data itself from the subjects. In addition, the ad hoc nature of continually adding and dropping of subjects at any point in time provides a unique research obstacle which in many instances simply can not be overcome.

To highlight some of the difficulties in collecting original data in a study such as this, the Dallas County Adult Probation Department had 44 clients on EM when the pretesting commenced with more EM offenders being added each week. Out of the 44 EM initial clients eligible to participate in the study, 25 (56.8%) volunteered to participate in the study. The Harris County Adult Probation Department had approximately 60 offenders in their EM program when pretesting began there, and 52 (86.7%) of those offenders agreed to participate in the study.

DEMOGRAPHIC DESCRIPTION OF THE ENTIRE SAMPLE

The vast majority of subjects in this study were offenders who had failed to succeed in either regular and/or intensive probation or parole programs. Initially, sentencing and parole guidelines were used in determining which clients had been selected as regular supervised probationers or as released parolees. The selection systems utilized risk assessment and offense severity criterion. Those offenders who rated high were placed on intensive supervision programs, rather than regular supervision. If the offender succeeds on the more intensive supervision programs, he/she is placed on a less restrictive program. If the offender fails on regular supervision and/or intensive supervision without EM, he/she may be placed on EM. Therefore, the EM clientele is predominately made up of those individuals who have failed at other programs. In essence, EM becomes the last resort next to prison.[1]

A total of 261 offenders were administered the test instruments. Fifty-three (53) subjects were on regular probation, 93 were on EM probation, 45 were on regular parole, and 70 were on EM parole of one sort or another. Overall, 85.0% of the subjects were males. Males constituted 76.9% of the subjects on regular probation, 82.8% of those on EM probation, 91.1% of those on regular parole and 90.0% of those on EM parole. Thus, females are slightly more likely to be found under traditional probation supervision than on EM or parole.

The majority of these 261 offenders (58.2%) ranged from 22 to 35 years of age, and there were more non-white offenders (53.1%) than white offenders (46.9%). The bulk of these offenders were single (59.2%), and most (44.8%) had less than 12 years of education. The offenses of the offenders ranged from property crimes (43.8%), to substance abuse crimes (41.7%), to crimes against the person (14.5%). Twenty-three point four percent (23.4%) of the offenders stated that they lived alone, 39.8% with one other person, and the remaining 36.8 with three or more persons. Forty-one point eight percent (41.8%) of those living with children, lived with from one to two children while the remaining 58.3% lived with three or more children. The preponderance of offenders (83.5%) professed to have a good relationship with their family.

Regarding drug and/or alcohol abuse prior to arrest, 31.1% indicated no abuse, 7.1% declared social drinking, 8.3% social use of drugs, and 21.3% social use of both alcohol and drugs. Of those claiming alcohol and/or drugs as being a serious problem, 7.1% claimed alcohol, 9.4% claimed drugs, and 15.7% reported both alcohol and drugs as a serious problem. For the majority of this population their current alcohol and/or drug abuse usage patterns have drastically changed. Eighty-four point two (84.2%) reported that they presently are non-users of both alcohol and drugs.

Most (50.8%) of these offenders had full time employment, and the majority (74.6%) reported working at unskilled jobs (i.e., unskilled, semi-skilled, or manual). The vast majority (83.8%) of the spouses of married offenders were unemployed. Thirty-five point seven percent (35.7%) of the spouses who were employed held clerical jobs, with the majority (42.8%) of the remainder holding unskilled ones.

DEMOGRAPHIC DESCRIPTION OF THE SUB-SAMPLES

The mean age of the sampled offenders was 27.9 years, with a standard deviation of 8.141. In all sub-groups the modal category was 22 to 35 years of age. This age group accounted for 48.1% of the regular probationers, 54.8% of the EM probationers, 60.0% of the regular parolees, and 70.0% of the EM parolees. Overall, 63 subjects were under 21 years of age, 152 were between 22 and 35 years (58.2%), and 44 were over age 35 (16.9%). Regular probationers had a mean age of 27.6 years, EM probationers averaged 26.9 years of age, regular parolees had an average age of 28.0 years and EM parolees had a mean age of 30.0 years. Oneway ANOVA results indicate that the EM parolees were, on average, significantly older than subjects in the other sub-group ($F = 4.48$; $P = 0.012$).

The sample consisted of 122 whites (46.9%), 108 blacks (41.5%), 28 Hispanics (10.7%) and two of other races, i.e., Native Americans and Asians (.8%). Regular probationers were disproportionately white (73.1%) with only five Hispanics (9.6%) and nine blacks (17.3%). Forty-nine point five percent (49.5%) of the EM probationers were white, 39.8% black and 9.7% Hispanic. The ratio of whites to blacks changes radically when parolees are examined. Sixty-eight point nine percent (68.9%) of the subjects on regular parole were black while only 17.8% were white. An additional 13.3% were Hispanic. Forty-two point nine percent (42.9%) of the EM parolees were black and 44.3% were white with an additional 11.4% Hispanic. This distribution corresponds, albeit roughly, to the distribution of ethnic groups in the general correctional population of Texas. Oneway ANOVA results indicate that race was a significant predictor of the type of supervision under which offenders were placed (F=11.271; P=0.000). The same data were also analyzed with race coded dichotomously as white or non-white and oneway ANOVA was again significant (F=14.455; P=0.000). Scheffe's procedure indicated that traditional probationers were distinctly more likely to be white than were members of any other sub-group. EM probationers were also significantly more often white than were those on regular parole supervision.

The average educational level of the total sample was just under 12 years (X = 11.134; S = 2.639). Regular probationers had an average educational level of 12.1 years (S = 1.987) while probationers on EM averaged 11.8 years (S = 1.871). Parolees on regular supervision had a mean educational level of 10.8 (S = 1.995) years while those on EM averaged 9.9 years (S = 3.358), 42.5% of the subjects had not completed high school, 37.9% were high school graduates, and 17.2% have had at least some college. Thirty-two point seven percent (32.7%) of the regular probationers did not have a high school diploma, while 30.8% had some college and 36.5% were high school graduates. Probationers on EM showed much the same distribution with 31.2% not having completed high school, 44.1% high school graduates and 24.7% having had some college.

When parolees are compared with probationers, the educational deficits traditionally associated with incarcerated offenders become prominent. Only 4.4% of subjects on regular parole had some college while 51.1% are high school drop-outs and 44.4% had twelve years of schooling. Sixty point zero percent (60.0%) of the EM parolees had not completed high school while 27.1% had a high school diploma, and only 5.7% had acquired college credits. The educational differences between parolees and probationers were statistically significant (F=13.425; P=0.000) with the parolees having more frequent deficits than the probationers.

The majority of the sample (59.0%) were single with only 27.2% married at the time of the study. Another 13.4% were separated, divorced or widowed (this group is hereafter referred to as "other" in terms of marital status). Probationers followed this pattern with 63.5% of the regular probationers and 55.9% of those on EM being single. Twenty-one point two percent (21.2%) of the regular probationers and 31.2% of the EM probationers were married, while 15.4% of the regular probationers and 12.9% of those on EM were classified as "other" on this variable. Parolees under regular supervision were even less likely than probationers to be married. Seventy-five point six (75.6%) of the regular parolees reported that they were single. However, only 50.0% of EM parolees were single while 31.4% were married, and 18.6% were widowed or divorced. Oneway ANOVA indicated that no significant differences in marital status existed between sub-groups (F=2.115; P=0.099).

When demographic variables were used to explicate the variance in type of supervision, the main effects (F=2.729; P=0.017) were statistically significant. However, the main effects on the linear model was significant due only to the effects of sex (F=6.647; P=0.011). Women were more likely to be probationers than parolees and less likely to be on EM than males. Education (F=2.465; P=0.090) was nearly significant. Neither age (F=1.657; P=0.196) nor marital status (F=0.646; P=0.423) had any discernible effects.

The study also examined the number of persons residing in the same household as the offender. The overall sample had an average household of 3.3 persons (S = 1.746). There was little difference across groups on this variable. Regular probationers had an average of 3.0 (S = 1.260) co-residents while those on EM had a mean household size of 3.4 (S = 1.695). Subjects under regular parole supervision had a mean of 3.6 (S = 2.156) while those on EM averaged 3.4 co-residents (S = 1.794). There were no significant differences in overall household size between the four sub-groups (F=0.214; P=0.887).

The typical household in this study had an average of 2.3 adults (S=1.079) and 1.1 children (S=1.282). Among regular probationers the typical household had 2.3 adults (S=1.126) and 0.7 children (S=0.875) while probationers on EM averaged 2.3 adults (S=0.938) and 1.1 children (S=1.374). Regular parolees lived in households with an average of 2.2 adults (S=1.506) and 1.4 children (S=1.470) while parolees on EM had a mean of 2.2 adult co-residents (S=1.358) and 1.2 children (S=1.227). There were no significant differences between subgroups on the number of adult co-residents (F=0.554; P=0.646). However, persons on regular parole supervision had significantly more children in their homes (F=3.238; P=0.228) than did members of other sub-groups.

Employment was measured on a three point scale ranging from unemployed to employed part-time and employed full-time. Fifty point two percent (50.2%) of the sample was employed part-time and 16.1% were employed full-time. Fifty-nine point six percent (59.6%) of the subjects on regular probation were employed part-time while another 21.2% were unemployed and 19.2% were employed full-time. EM probationers were similarly distributed with 28.0% unemployed, 54.8% employed part time and 17.2% employed full time. Fifty seven point eight percent (57.8%) of the subjects on regular parole and 34.3% of those on EM parole were unemployed at the time of the study. This discrepancy is likely due to the fact that many of the EM parolees were on pre-parole transfer status in which employment is mandatory for inclusion in the program. Only 8.9% of those on regular parole and 17.1% of those on EM parole were employed full time while 33.3% of the regular parolees and 48.6% of the EM parolees were employed part-time. The greater likelihood of employment among probationers, regardless of the type of supervision they were under, was statistically significant (F=5.537; P=0.004).

Occupational status was measured on Hollingshead's seven point scale[2] ranging from the unskilled through executives. The mean occupational level of the sample was 1.9 (S=2.05) or semiskilled (2.0). Probationers tended to have occupations of a skilled nature   whether on regular supervision (X=2.034; S=2.14) or EM (X=2.38; S=2.192). Parolees on regular supervision had the lowest mean occupational levels in the sample with a mean of 1.0 (S=1.69) while EM parolees had a mean level of 1.7 (S=1.741). Of the employed probationers most were in unskilled (31%) or semi-skilled (15.5%) positions. Probationers on EM, however, tended to have either unskilled (16%) or skilled manual jobs (19%) when employed. White collar occupations at the level of management and administration accounted for 3.4% of the regular probationers and 4% of the EM probationers.

Among regular parolees with jobs, most were in unskilled (10.9%) or semi-skilled (10.9%) positions. Only one (2.2%) parolee claimed to hold a clearly white collar position. Nine point one percent (9.1%) of the EM parolees held unskilled positions and another 10.6% held semi-skilled jobs. However, 24.2% of the EM parolees were in clerical or sales positions and 13.7% held managerial positions or better. The average occupational level of EM probationers was significantly higher than that of the other three sub-groups (F=5.439; P=0.001).

The study also queried respondents as to their substance abuse and criminal histories. Substance abuse was classified as drug and/or alcohol oriented. Subjects were asked to describe their use as social or serious. The sample was distributed in a tri-modal fashion with most subjects claiming not to have been drug or alcohol abusers (33.3%), but over one-fifth (20.7%) admitted to social use of both drugs and alcohol while 15.3% admitted to serious problems with both drugs and alcohol. Thirty point eight percent (30.8%) of the regular probationers claimed to be non-users prior to their arrest while 13.5% admitted to the social use of drugs and 5.8% to the social use of alcohol prior to their arrest. Twenty one point two percent (21.2%) of this group admitted to serious drug use histories while an additional 13.5% claimed to have had serious alcohol problems, and 13.5% claimed to have abused both alcohol and drugs in a serious fashion. In comparison, EM probationers seemed somewhat more likely to be social rather than serious users of psychoactive substances.

Thirty-three point three percent (33.3%) of this group claimed to be non-users while 15.1% admitted to social drug use and 8.6% to social use of alcohol. Ten point eight percent (10.8%) used both in a social manner. Fourteen point zero percent (14.0%) of the EM probationers admitted to having had a serious pattern of drug use prior to their arrest but only 6.5% admitted to a serious drinking problem. Eleven point eight percent (11.8%) had used both alcohol and drugs in a serious fashion.

Persons under parole supervision were more homogeneous in their distribution on this variable than were probationers. Forty point zero percent (40.0%) claimed not to have used either type of substance prior to being incarcerated. An additional 33.3% admitted to using both drugs and alcohol in a social manner and 24.4% admitted having had serious problems with both prior to incarceration, and only one parolee on regular supervision admitted to an alcohol problem (2.2%). EM parolees were equally homogeneous but somewhat more likely to have been substance-involved than their counterparts on regular supervision. Twenty-eight point six percent (28.6%) claimed to be non-users but the majority (40.0%) admitted to the social use of both types of substances. Only 15.7% of this group admitted to having had serious problems with both prior to incarceration. However, differences between subgroups in admitted substance abuse patterns were not statistically discernible from zero (F=0.397; P=0.755).

The offenses for which the subject was currently under sentence were coded as substance abuse, property crimes or crimes against persons, in ascending order of relative seriousness. The sample mean was 1.6 (S=1.05) or midway between substance abuse and property crimes. The modal category was property crimes (39.5%), closely followed by substance abuse offenses (37.5%). The remaining 13.0% had been convicted of crimes against persons. Non-EM probationers appeared to more often be involved in serious crimes (X=1.885, S=1.114) than their EM counterparts (X=1.581, S=0.981). This distinction was statistically significant (F=4.634; P=0.004). Among regular probationers the majority were property offenders (42.3%) or had committed offenses related to substance abuse (34.6%). Twenty-three point one percent (23.1%) of this sub-group had been convicted of crimes against persons. The majority of EM probationers were substance abusers (54.8%). Property offenders accounted for another 32.3% of this group and crimes against persons involved only 12.9% of these subjects.

Regular parolees had much the same pattern of offense types as those on traditional probation. The majority were property offenders (51.1%) but substance abuse offenses were more common (15.6%) than were crimes against persons (11.1%) in this sub-group. Missing data was more frequent among parolees and, along with unclassifiable responses, accounted for 22.2% of the data in this group. Missing data was also common among the parolees on EM (21.4%). Property offenders were again the modal category (40.0%) followed by substance abuse charges (31.4%) and then crimes against persons (7.1%).

PRE-BECK DEPRESSION INVENTORY (BDI) RESULTS

The study employed two psychometric instruments: the Beck Depression Inventory (BDI) and the Family Environment Scale (FES), to measure the relative well-being of the subjects. Each of these instruments were discussed in detail in the previous Chapter. The BDI and the FES were given to the offenders and their spouses at two different points in time in this study. The first tests, here identified as Pre-BDI and Pre-FES, were given approximately at the time the offender was placed on (hooked-up to) EM; and the second or subsequent tests, here identified as Post-BDI and Post-FES, were administered approximately 90 days after the pretests.

The BDI is scored in a cumulative fashion with a range of possible scores ranging from zero (0) to fifty-one (51). The overall sample had a mean BDI score of 9.345 (S=7.850) which is just beyond the normal range. Subjects on regular probation had the lowest average score (X=7.731; S=6.704) while EM probationers averaged 10.032 (S=8.119). Regular parolees had a mean BDI score of 8.644 (S=8.345) while EM parolees averaged 9.914 (S=7.838). There were no significant differences between sub-groups on the BDI (F=0.859; P=0.463).

The great majority of the sample fell within the normal (58.2%) or mildly depressed (25.3%) range of the BDI. Five point seven percent (5.7%) were classified as "mildly to moderately depressed" and 7.7% were "moderately to severely" depressed. Only eight subjects (3.1%) were severely depressed according to the initial BDI results. These severely depressed offenders were spread throughout the four sub-groups. One was on regular probation, three were on EM probation, one was on regular parole and two were on EM parole. The same pattern was found in each sub-group except for EM parolees where 15.8% (N=11) reported being moderately to severely depressed.

PRE-FAMILY ENVIRONMENT SCALE (FES) RESULTS

As discussed in Chapter 7, the FES is divided into three dimensions which are measured by ten sub-scales. The first dimension, Relationship, is measured by the cohesiveness, expressiveness, and conflict scales. The next dimension of Personal Growth (goal orientation) is measured by the independence, achievement orientation, intellectual-cultural orientation, active-recreational orientation, and moral-religious emphasis scales. The third and last dimension, System Maintenance, is measured in terms of the organization and control scales. Each of these areas is scored and gives an indication of the perceived family environment based on the clients' answers to the true/false statements.

Complicating the FES analysis is the fact that because of administrative and logistical difficulties, probationers were administered the entire FES but parolees were asked to complete only two sub-scales: those measuring control and conflict within the home. The conflict sub-scale assesses the amount of anger, aggression and conflict among family members; and the control sub-scale measures the extent to which rules and procedures are used to run family life.[3] Precedents for using selected subscales of the FES can be found in Ford, Bashford, and DeWitt's[4] work with marital communication training in which they utilized FES Cohesion and Expressiveness subscales, and Boss'[5] use of six of the FES subscales with families of missing servicemen.

It should be noted that some of the following interpretations of the statistics provided in this report are based on the scoring nature of the FES subscales. Unlike many psychometric tests the FES utilizes a mean score as the ideal or best score, rather than the more conventional use of a low or high score, as the ideal or best score. The FES subscales have a scoring range of 0.0 to 9.0. These scores are subdivided into continuum range scores of 0.0 to 5.0, with a score of 0.0 indicating the largest amount of under control/conflict and 5.0 indicating a normal amount of control/conflict. Similarly, subscale scores range from 9.0 to 5.0. A score of 9.0 indicates the largest amount of over control/conflict while a score of 5.0 indicates the normal amount of control/conflict. Thus, subscale scores near 5.0 are interpreted as the normal amount of family control/conflict to be found in normal families. In the analysis which follows the writers have elected to interpret subscale scores below 4.0 and over 6.0 as indicating a dysfunctional amount of intrafamilial control/conflict. In essence, 0.0 to 4.0 is the scoring range being used for identifying too little or too much intrafamilial control/conflict, and 9.0 to 6.0 the scoring range indicating progressively higher amounts of over control.

Pretest results show that this sample of offenders averaged a raw score of 2.452 (S=2.142) on the conflict scale. Among subjects on regular probation supervision, conflict sub-scale scores averaged 2.3456 (S= 2.057) while EM probationers had a mean conflict score of 2.527 (S=2.104). Those on regular parole supervision had an average conflict score of 2.956 (S=2.153) while EM parolees averaged 2.043 (S=2.156). Thus, all four sub-groups show a lower than normal amount of conflict within their families, with EM parole families having the least and regular parole families the most. These differences, however, are not statistically significant (F=1.795; P=0.148).

Control scale scores averaged 4.828 (S=1.856) for the entire sample, 4.769 (S=1.906) among regular probationers and 5.043 among EM probationers (S=1.654). Subjects on traditional parole supervision had a mean control score of 5.000 (S=1.523) while those on EM averaged 4.486 (S=2.225). All four subgroups were found to be exerting the normal amount of family control, with EM probationer families exerting the most and EM parole families the least. However, oneway ANOVA indicated that there were no significant differences between the subgroups within our sample on the control scale (F=1.358; P=0.256).

Attention is finally directed at three dimensions of the FES: Relationship, Personal Growth, and System Maintenance. These dimensions serve to summarize overall FES scores but are available only for probationers. The relationship dimension is composed of the cohesion, expressiveness and conflict sub-scales. The sampled probationers had a mean of 14.510 (2.821) on this dimension. Those on traditional supervision averaged 14.865 (S=3.036) while those on EM had a mean of 14.312 (S=2.690). The personal growth dimension is composed of the independence and achievement-orientation sub-scales. This sample of probationers had an overall mean of 29.110 (S=5.849). Those on traditional supervision averaged 29.346 (S=5.083) while those on EM had a mean of 28.978 (S=6.259). The system maintenance dimension is composed of the organization and control sub-scales. The mean for all probationers was 11.324 (S=2.948) on this dimension with those on traditional supervision averaging 10.769 (S=3.473) and those on EM averaging 11.643 (S=2.578). Oneway ANOVA indicated that there were no significant differences between sub-groups on any of these FES variables. Thus, the sub-groups can be said to follow the same pattern on each of the psychometric instruments employed in this research.

EXPLICATION OF PRETEST RESULTS

Complete FES results for the entire ten subscales for the three dimensions of the FES are available only for probationers; therefore, only offenders in these groups are used in analyses of the three dimensions or complete FES. When the effects of demographic variables on the relationship dimension were analyzed using ANOVA, none were found to be of significance ($F=1.087$, $P=.385$). Only educational level ($F=3.302; P=0.045$) attained statistical significance in explicating the variance in responses to the growth dimension (Main effects $F=1.607$; $P=0.145$). Since education is one method by which the individual learns to adapt to the surrounding world, the significance of this variable is not surprising. Results for the system maintenance scale were similar to those for the relationship dimension - none of the demographic variables had an effect that was statistically discernible from zero ($F=0.737$; $P=0.641$).

Because they are: (1) especially critical to the central question being investigated; and (2) available for all groups of respondents, the control and conflict scales were given much attention at this stage of analysis. ANOVA was first used to estimate the effects of social environment and pretest BDI scores on these two FES scales for all offenders ($N=261$). Respondents were divided into EM and non-EM groups to create a new independent variable. In addition, the BDI scores, educational levels, regularity of employment of offenders and the presence/absence of EM supervision were used in this analysis.

Only the BDI score had a significant impact ($F=8.691$; $P=0.000$) on the control scale. The significance of the main effects ($F=4.617$; $P=0.000$) is attributable to the impact of this variable. When the effects of these four variables on the control scale were estimated with ANOVA, the main effects were nearly significant ($F=1.939$; $P=0.058$) as was the impact of the BDI pretest score ($F=2.218$; $P=0.069$). However, the regularity of the offender's employment had an effect that was statistically significant ($F=4.015; P=0.047$). One plausible explanation for this finding is that, in general, employment is normally viewed as influencing the level of control within households by helping to establish an economic hierarchy. Since most of our respondents are males, it is likely that the regularity with which they maintain employment directly effects the degree of control they are able to exercise within the family.

When the conflict scale was examined, only the offender's level of education was found to approach statistical significance ($F=2.682$; $P=0.073$). The main effects were not significant ($F=1.785$; $P=0.110$). However, no other variable even remotely approached significance. The significance of education to reported level of conflict probably reflects the acquisition of problem-solving skills by the more educated families. An identical analysis of control scale scores indicated that none of these variables had an effect on this measure that was discernible from zero (Main Effects: $F=0.924$; $P=0.481$.

Regression, a more powerful analytical procedure, was used to explicate the joint effects of nine independent variables on control and conflict pretest scores. Two stepwise regressions were required, one for each dependent variable, using sex, age, education, marital status, number of adults and children in the home, employment, pre-BDI score and the type of supervision the offender was under (i.e., EM or non-EM) as independent or predictor variables. It can be noted in passing the R^2 indicates the amount of variance in the dependent variable that is explicated by the independent variables; F tests the hypothesis of no linear relationship between independent and dependent variables and is associated with the R^2. Beta or standardized regression coefficients suggest the importance of each independent variable in explicating the dependent variable while controlling for all other independent variables. T values test the hypothesis that there is no linear relationship between the independent variable and the dependent variable and thus clarify the significance of the Beta weights.

When conflict pretest scores were examined, the first variable entered into the equation was the offender's pre-BDI score ($F=24.167$; $P=.000$). This variable explained nearly ten percent of the variance in conflict scores ($R^2=0.082$). Age was entered on the second step and increased the explanatory power of the regression equation to 14% ($R^2=.137$, $F=21.556$; $P=0.000$). On the model's third iteration, the offender's substance abuse history was entered to produce an R^2 of 0.177 ($F=19.664$; $P=.000$). The final variable to achieve significance in this equation was the type of offense for which the offender was last convicted ($R^2=.196$; $F=16.821$ $P=.000$). Thus the model presented here can be said to have explained nearly one-fifth of the variance in conflict pretest scores with these four variables. In the final model used to explain conflict scale scores the offender's BDI score was the best single predictor with a Beta weight of .276 ($t=4.899$,$P=.000$). Age was nearly as powerful, however, with a Beta weight of -.246 ($t=-4362$;$P=.000$) though it appears to operate in the opposite direction as the BDI score. Substance abuse history is the next most important variable in this model (Beta=0.211; $t=3.793$; $P=.0002$) followed by the type of offense for which the offender was convicted (Beta=.142; $t=2.632$; $P=.009$). Since depression can be interpreted as either a cause or result of conflict within the home, its significant impact on this FES sub-scale is not surprising. Ageing is, usually, viewed as increasing personal identification with the family unit and to assist in establishing an appropriate perspective on the relative importance of various aspects of life. Therefore, its inverse association with conflict is also to be expected. The fact that conflict increases with substance abuse is also to be expected, since a history of substance abuse implies that chemical dependency has eroded the offender's loyalty to the family and left a history of aberrant behavior that can only be overcome with time and positive behavior. The more serious the crime committed by the offender, the more dysfunctional that person can be assumed to be. The presence of dysfunctional persons, especially in positions of power in the family hierarchy, is more likely to increase the conflict in the home.

The first variable to be entered in the parallel equation for control scale scores was the offender's sex ($R^2 = .017$; $F = 5.375$; $P = 0.021$) which explicated just over 1.0% of the variance in the dependent variable. The offender's educational level was next entered and increased the R^2 to 0.032 ($F = 5.337$; $P = .005$). Abuse history was then entered into the equation ($R^2 = .047$; $F = 5.246$; $P = 0.002$) followed by the offender's employment status ($R^2 = .06$; $F = 5.062$; $P = .001$). The offense that resulted in the offender's last conviction was the last variable found to have a significant impact on control scale scores. This linear model explained 7.0% of the variance in the dependent variable ($R^2 = .070$; $F = 4.921$; $P = .000$).

While the model of control scale scores included more variables than that for the conflict scores, its explanatory power is much less. This model's reliance on demographic variables raises suspicions of collinearity between independent variables which is likely to be moderately high and renders causal interpretation highly problematic.[6] The offender's educational level (Beta = -1.68; t = -2.761; P = .006) appeared to have the most explanatory power followed by sex (Beta = -.161; t = -2.661; P = .008), substance abuse history (Beta = -2.216; t = -2.216; P = .028), employment status (Beta = -.128; t = -2.144; P = .033) and type of offense (Beta = .123; t = 2.028; P = .044). The same explanations offered for the results of the demographic variables on conflict scores would appear to apply here also.

POSTTEST RESULTS FOR THE BDI

The mean score for the entire sample on the BDI was 3.9 ($S = 7.030$). The great majority of offenders were not dysphoric according to this measure (85.8%). Seven point three percent (7.3%) had BDI scores indicating mild depression, 1.9% fell into the mild-to-moderate category, 3.1% were in the moderately dysphoric category and the remaining 1.9% were classified as severely depressed.

Among offenders on traditional probation supervision the average BDI score was 5.8. Again, most of these subjects were not dysphoric according to the BDI (78.8%). Eleven point five percent (11.5%) were mildly depressed, while only 1.9% were in the mild-to-moderate category and 3.8% were in both the moderate and severe categories.

Probationers on EM were similarly distributed. They had a mean BDI score of 5.6 (S=8.020) and the great majority did not appear to be dysphoric (79.6%). Ten point eight percent (10.8%) were classified as mildly dysphoric with only 1.1% in the mild-to-moderate group and 2.2% in the severely dysphoric category. However, 6.5% were classified as moderately dysphoric by this instrument.

Parolees on traditional supervision averaged 3.1 on the BDI (S=7.285). A lack of dysphoria was somewhat more common among these offenders (88.9%) than among the probationers. None of these subjects fell into the moderately dysphoric grouping but 4.4% were categorized as mildly dysphoric or mildly-to-moderately so. Only 2.2% of these offenders were severely dysphoric. Parolees on EM had the least dysphoria of any group examined (X=0.686; S=2.635). Virtually all (97.1%) of these subjects were in the non-dysphoric category with only 1.4% in the mild and mild-to-moderate groupings.

Oneway ANOVA indicated that the type of supervision an offender was under had a significant effect on his/her BDI posttest score (F=9.040; P=.0000). Scheffe's procedure clarified this distinction by identifying the significant differential between both categories of probationers and EM parolees. This procedure indicated that parolees on traditional supervision were not statistically different from either probationers or EM parolees. However, the EM parolees had a posttest BDI mean that was significantly lower than that of either group of probationers. Since EM parolees are in most cases considered marginal candidates for release from prison, this finding is not particularly surprising.

Stepwise regression was used to explicate the effects of offender demographics, type of supervision, presence of EM, type of offense, and substance abuse history on posttest BDI scores. The type of supervision was the first variable to be entered into the equation and produced an R^2 of .083 (F=24.613; P=.0000). The offender's age was the next variable entered and its addition to the model resulted in an R^2 of .113 (F=17.448; P=.0000). Type of offense was the last variable to be successfully entered and produced an R^2 of .125 for the model (F=13.297; P=.000). This is to say that knowledge of an offender's type of supervision, age, and type of offense explained 12.5% of the variance in BDI posttest scores.

The type of supervision had a Beta weight of -.308 (t=-5.156; P=.000) while the Beta for age was -.184 (t=3.156; P=.002) and the Beta associated with type of offense was -.127 (t=-2.126; P=.035). None of the other variables had an impact on posttest BDI scores that was discernible from zero. The negative sign associated with these Beta weights indicates that post BDI scores were most likely to decrease as type of supervision became more rigorous. The fact that parolees were less depressed than probationers is logical since they have recently been released from institutional custody whereas probationers have, for the most part, not previously experienced direct legal controls on their lives. Younger offenders are also logically associated with higher levels of dysphoria because they are less likely to have encountered the criminal justice system and because of the fewer responsibilities they have encountered in life. Since offense type and type of supervision are causally related in an obvious fashion a collinearity problem exists in that the effects of type of crime and type of supervision cannot be estimated independent of one another. Thus, the same factors used to explain the effects of type of supervision can be applied to the offender's age.

POSTTEST RESULTS FOR THE FES

The overall posttest sample mean for the conflict scale of the FES was 1.1 (S=1.822). Eighty-one point six percent (81.6%) had scores in the lowest third of the possible range. Only 1.6% of the offenders reported levels of conflict in their families that were in the top third of the possible range of scores. The sample mean for the posttest control scale scores was 2.3 (S=2.811). Fifty-seven point nine percent (57.9%) of the offenders had control scale scores in the lowest third of the possible range, 32.9% were in the middle ranges of the scale and the remaining 9.2% were at the high end of this scale.

Traditional probationers had a mean conflict scale score of 1.8 (S=2.168) while EM probationers averaged 1.419 (S=1.820). Non-EM parolees averaged 1.0 (S=1.989) on this measure while their EM counterparts had a conflict scale mean of 0.243 (S=.875). Oneway ANOVA indicated that the differences between the means of the four groups under different types of supervision was significant (F=9.220; P=.0000). Scheffe's procedure demonstrated that EM parolees had an average conflict scale score that was considerably less than those of both types of probationers. Familial conflicts undoubtedly pale in comparison with those encountered in prison. Thus, the parolee's with the greatest likelihood of returning to prison are likely to see conflicts at home as less severe than others. It may also be that they make a greater effort to avoid conflict, either as a "holdover" survival strategy from prison or as a method of partially insuring successful completion of parole.

Control scale scores among probationers not on EM averaged 3.3 (S = 2.871) while EM probationers had a mean of 3.4 (S = 2.801). Parolees on traditional supervision had a mean posttest score of 1.6 (S = 2.589) while EM parolees averaged 0.5 (S = 1.421). Oneway ANOVA indicated a significant difference (F = 24.689; P = .0000) among group means on this variable. Scheffe's procedure showed that significant differences between probationers and parolees were discernible on this variable regardless of the presence or absence of EM within these categories. Because they are older parolees are less likely to fall easily under familial control and this is apparent in their FES scores on this sub-scale. The lower level of reported familial control is also a likely contributor to the extremely low conflict scores of this group.

Stepwise regression was used to estimate the effects of EM, BDI posttest scores, age, sex, education, employment status, marital status, and household composition variables on posttest conflict scores. The first variable to be successfully entered into this equation was the BDI posttest score (R^2 = .258; F = 91.077; P = .000). The employment status of the offender was entered next and increased the model's R^2 to .270 (F = 48.908; P = .000). The presence of EM supervision was the last variable to be successfully entered into this regression equation and resulted in a final R^2 of .281 (F = 34.674; P = .000). Beta weights for both the BDI score (.514; t = 9.20; P = .000) and employment status (.129; t = 2.453; P = .015) were positive, indicating a positive linear relationship. The Beta weight for the presence of EM supervision was negative (-.116; t = -2.184; P = .031) indicating that conflict scores were, on average, higher in non-EM families.

The fact that dysphoria had a direct and positive effect on familial conflict is to be expected although these data do not allow us to speculate as to whether dysphoria is a cause or an effect of conflict. The positive association of the regularity of an offender's employment with conflict in the home is difficult to explain. Indeed, quite the opposite direction was expected for this Beta. It may be that the more an offender works, the more he/she expects in terms of obedient gratitude from the family. Since offenders can be characterized as dysfunctional humans, such expectations would be conflict producing, especially in the context of a history that includes direct or indirect abuse of family members and/or responsibilities by the offender. The impact of EM on reported perceptions of family conflict is noteworthy in this context since the analysis indicates that presence of EM is associated with low levels of friction within the family. Because this relationship did not attain significance when pretest data were analyzed the data suggest that EM may have a positive effect in this regard.

When the same regression procedure was used to explicate the variance in control scale posttest scores somewhat different results were obtained. The BDI post test was entered first with an R^2 of .128 (F=39.031; P=.000). Marital status was entered into the equation on the second and final iteration resulting in an R^2 of .141 (F=22.337; P=.000) for the model. The Beta weight for the BDI post test (.374) was significant (t=6.474; P=.000), indicating the presence of a direct linear relationship between dysphoria and perceived control by the family. The Beta for marital status (.130) also indicates a significant, direct linear relationship (t=2.243; P=.026) of less magnitude.

High control scores, in conjunction with correctional supervision could be expected to result in dysphoria due to the offenders's perception of being over-controlled. Such dual-controls may not always be congruent in their demands on the offender and the assignment of supremacy to one set will, in most cases, lead to conflicts with the other. The direct relationship between marital status and control was expected since spouses are more likely to be intimate with, and dependent upon, one another than would parents or other co-habitants.

EXPLICATION OF PRE-TO-POST CHANGES

The crucial variable in this study was the change in psychometric scores between the pretest and posttests. The mean change for all subjects on the BDI was +2.2 (S=6.734). In the overall sample 0.4% of the subjects's BDI scores dropped by four points, 2.3% dropped by two points and another 2.3% decreased by one point. Sixty-two point eight percent (62.8%) of the sample showed no change in BDI score. Twenty point seven percent (20.7%) had an increase of one point on this measure while 3.8% showed an increase of two points, 6.5% increased by three points and 1.1% increased by four points.

Offenders on traditional probation showed the largest net increase of 4.3 (S=7.275). The scores of EM probationers rose an average of 3.9 (S=7.438) while parolees on traditional supervision showed an increase of only 1.5 (S=6.904) and those on EM exhibited a decrease of 1.1 (S=2.981). Oneway ANOVA indicated that EM parolees were statistically discernible from both groups of probationers.

Stepwise regression was used to estimate the impact of demographic variables, household size, and employment status on the amount of change between the pretest and posttest scores of the BDI. The offender's age was the first variable to be entered in this equation (R^2=.037; F=10.043; P=.002). Education was the next and last variable to be successfully entered (R^2=.057;

$F=8.817$; $P=.000$). The change in R^2 that resulted from the addition of education (.027) was significant according to the associated F-ratio (F change $=7.345$; $P=.007$). The Beta weight associated with age was -.201 ($t=-3.329$; $P=.001$), indicating that as the offender's age increases, dysphoria tends to decrease over time during community supervision. Much the same relationship exists between education and (Beta $=.164$; $t=2.710$; $P=.007$) change in dysphoria over time, though to a lesser extent. The fact that increases in age and education are associated with better, or quicker, acclimation to home confinement is not surprising since both lead to improved comprehension of social limitations and the value of the family as a social unit.

The difference between pretest and posttest control scale scores were next analyzed. The overall sample showed a decrease of 1.3 ($S=2.390$). Three point eight percent (3.8%) of the sample had posttest scores that were three to four points lower than their pretest. Twelve point six percent (12.6%) showed decreases of one to two points. Twenty-three point four percent (23.4%) showed no change. Thirty-three point four percent (33.4%) showed an increase in conflict scores of one to two points, another 16.2% showed an increase of three to four points, and 10.8% showed an increase of five to nine points.

Probationers on traditional supervision averaged a decrease of 0.6 points ($S=2.060$) on the conflict scale while their EM counterparts had a mean decrease of 1.1 points ($S=2.487$). Parolees on regular supervision had an average decrease of 2.0 ($S=2.374$) while those on EM averaged 1.8 points less on the post test than they had on the pretest ($S=2.357$). Oneway ANOVA indicated that differences between these four groups were significant ($F=3.955$; $P=.009$). Scheffe's procedure indicated that probationers on regular supervision were statistically distinct from both groups of parolees on this measure of change in perceived familial conflict over the testing period.

Stepwise regression was used to explore the effects of demographic and household size variables on changes in conflict scale scores. Changes in BDI scores and the presence of EM were also included in this analysis as independent variables. Change in the BDI score was the first variable to be entered into this equation and it produced an R^2 of .106 ($F=31.556$; $P=.000$). The offender's age was the next variable to be entered and resulted in an R^2 of .140 ($F=21.994$; $P=.000$). The offender's marital status was the last variable to be successfully entered, resulting in an R^2 of .150 ($F=16.228$; $P=.000$) for the final model. The Beta weights for each of these three significant independent variables were positive. The change in BDI score had the most apparent impact (Beta $=.337$; $t=5.881$; $P=.000$), followed by that for age (Beta

=.152; t=2.507; P=.013) and finally by the Beta for marital status (.124; t=2.038; P=.043). It can be inferred from this analysis that increases in the level of reported familial conflict are associated with increases in dysphoria, age, and marriage in offenders. Marriage probably increases conflict because of the greater intimacy and investment it implies relative to other types of relationships. The predictive value of age may be due to the realization that much of one's life has been wasted on criminal, or at least deviant, pursuits.

Changes in control scale scores were the last to be analyzed. The sample had an overall decrease in control scale scores of 2.5 (S=3.136). Five point four percent (5.4%) reported a decrease of three to four points on this measure, 14.1% showed a decrease of one to two points, while 10.3% reported no change. Twenty-one point four percent (21.4%) showed an increase of one to two points, 16.5% showed an increase of three to four points, 23.0% increased by five to six points, and 9.2% increased by seven to nine points.

Probationers on regular supervision showed an average decrease of 1.2 (S=3.098) while those on EM had a mean decrease of 1.7 (S=2.987). Parolees on regular supervision had an average decrease in control scale score of 3.4 (S=2.904) while those on EM averaged a decline of 4.0 (S=2.659) points. Oneway ANOVA demonstrated that the differences between group means were significant (F=14.083; P=.000) and Scheffe's procedure indicated that the difference between those offenders on EM and those under traditional supervision outweighed distinctions between probationers and parolees.

Stepwise regression was again used to explicate the impact of changes in the BDI score and demographic and household variables on changes in control scale scores. As with the conflict scale changes, the BDI pretest-posttest change was the first variable to be entered into the equation (R^2=.084; F=24.665; P=.000). The employment status of the offender was the next, and last, variable to be entered into this equation, producing an R^2 for the final model of .108 (F=16.664; P=.000). The presence of EM did not appear to have a significant impact on control scale changes but its effect may have been masked by collinearity with other, more powerful, predictors of changes in perceived familial control. The role of employment status and dysphoria in predicting familial control is likely similar to that in predicting conflict.

In closing the discussion of pretest-posttest changes, it should be noted that the effects of EM are notably absent. Age, marital status, employment status and prior imprisonment seem to play a role in predicting changes in psychometric test scores over approximately three month periods of time but EM does not appear to have any discernible effect.

PREDICTION OF SUCCESSFUL COMPLETION OF COMMUNITY SUPERVISION

In the Table that follows, the distribution of offenders across combinations of EM and Success categories is displayed. With Yates' correction for a two-by-two table, EM's effects approach statistical significance (Chi Square = 3.201, P = .073). Examination of cell frequencies indicates that offenders on EM had a high rate of success (76.3%), however non-EM clients were more frequently successful (87.7) than those on monitoring. This is best attributed to the fact that the vast majority of clients assigned to EM have had problems in complying with the conditions of their initial release on regular community supervision. Thus, EM clients, as "difficult" clients who have failed on regular supervision, when compared to "non-difficult" clients who have not failed on regular community supervision, appear almost as likely to succeed.

TABLE: DISTRIBUTION OF SUCCESS ACROSS TYPES OF SUPERVISION

	Non-EM .00	EM 1.00	Row Total
Unsuccessful	8 26.7 12.3	22 73.3 23.7	30 19.0
Successful	57 44.5 87.7	71 55.5 76.3	128 81.0
Column Total	65 41.1	93 58.9	158 100.0

In order to further analyze the predictive utility of the psychometric results found on the successful completion of community supervision two major constraints on the analytical technique had to be dealt with. First, many of the preceding analyses indicate that differences between parolees and probationers are of greater import than those between offenders on traditional community and those on EM. For this reason three analyses, one for each category of supervision and one for the entire sample, are required. Secondly, the dependent or outcome variable in this case is a dichotomy - offenders were either successful in their completion of community supervision or they were not. Standard regression cannot be interpreted with any certainty when the dependent variable is coded in such a fashion. Therefore we have elected to use logistic regression which was designed to deal with just such a contingency.

The first logistic regression addressed the success of probationers using the difference between the pretest and posttest scores on the BDI, the control and conflict scales of the FES and the presence of EM as independent variables. This model made correct predictions of success in 91.27% of the cases. Three point one percent (3.9%) of the offenders were erroneously predicted to be failures when, in fact, they had successfully completed community supervision while 4.8% of the offenders were misclassified as successes when they had failed to complete community supervision successfully.

The pretest to posttest change in control scale scores had the most predictive power $(R = .326)$ and indicates that chances of success are directly related to the decline of perceived family control during electronic monitoring. The change in BDI score was also significant in the same direction $(R = .126)$. The impact of EM was next in importance and explained nearly 5.0% $(R = -.042)$ of the variance in failure. Changes in conflict scale scores $(R = .000)$ did not appear to have any measurable impact on successful completion of community supervision. Overall measures of this model's goodness of fit indicate that these predictor variables, taken together, have an effect that is statistically significant (Model: Chi Square = 55.128; P = .000).

The reported decline in family control over the period of the study, accompanied by the significant impact of EM, is of great substantive significance. These results imply that EM may serve to relieve the family of some of its control responsibilities. This may explain the decline in dysphoria since the replacement of controls associated with the family by correctional authorities (i.e., EM) provides the offender with a highly structured lifestyle but keeps the responsibility for its imposition outside the family unit. Thus, the effects of EM may well be beneficial for the offender as well as for the family with which he/she lives.

The same model was used to explain successful completion of supervision among the parolees in this sample. As has been previously noted, data for parolees is less often complete, resulting in a smaller number of cases amenable to multi-variate analyses. This diminution of the sample is likely to introduce selection biases that cannot be predicted. Therefore, analyses of parolees are much more tentative than those for probationers. For this group of subjects the model's fit is much weaker (model Chi Square = 25.318; P = .000) but still significant. The model made correct predictions in 90.63%

of the cases; 6.3% of the offenders were erroneously predicted to be failures when, in fact, they had successfully completed community supervision while 3.1% of the offenders were misclassified as successes when they had failed to complete community supervision successfully. One fourth of the parolees were correctly predicted to be failures and 65.6% were correctly predicted to be successes by these variables. Only the change in control scale score had an impact that was discernible from zero in this model however $(R = -.2541)$. Thus, it would appear that, for these subjects, the reduction of perceived familial control predicted success on community supervision, though to a smaller degree than for probationers. Although EM was not significant in this regression, its effects may be indirect and biases in the sub-sample due to missing data may be responsible for its lack of statistical significance.

When the entire sample is examined in this fashion, the predictive power of the independent variables falls to 89.87%. In addition, 4.43% were falsely classified as failures when in fact they successfully completed community supervision while 5.70% were classified as successes when they in fact were terminated before the end of their sentence. Changes in control scale scores were most prominent among the predictor variables $(R = .3584)$ but the presence of EM $(R = -.0733)$ and changes in dysphoria $(R = .0250)$ also had a measurable impact. These results are virtually the same as those for the parolees but the strength of the relationship between reduced perception of familial control and successful completion of supervision is stronger.

SUMMARY OF SIGNIFICANT ANALYTICAL RESULTS

In terms of differences between the analytical sub-groups within the sample several distinctions must be initially noted. Parolees on EM are significantly older than members of the other three groups. Probationers not on EM are significantly more likely to be white than members of any other group. Parolees, regardless of the type of supervision they are under are less well-educated than probationers of either type. Parolees, as a group, also have significantly more children in their households than do probationers. Probationers of both types are more likely to be employed than are either type of parolees. However, EM probationers show a significant tendency towards better jobs than do probationers under traditional supervision or either group of parolees.

None of the offender background variables examined predicted noteworthy differences in pretest BDI scores. The same is true of all the FES pretest measures examined except the growth dimension in which the subject's educational level had a significant impact. This finding is of little consequence however, since it was to be expected and is of little relevance to the efficacy of correctional treatments.

The subject's BDI score, age, substance abuse history, and type of offense had significant predictive power in regard to pretest conflict scores. The sex, educational level, substance abuse history, employment status and type of offense also had significant predictive power with regard to pretest control scores. None of these relationships was particularly surprising and virtually all of them could have been predicted from past research. None of them can be used to imply a problematic selection bias in the use of EM. As would be expected, differences between parolees and probationers are often greater than those between EM and non-EM groups. EM did not appear to have any predictive power with regard to any of the psychometric pretest measures. Thus, it can be inferred that the psychological states measured by these instruments (i.e., the BDI and FES subscales) are not a significant fact in selecting offenders for EM.

When posttest results are surveyed, EM parolees report significantly less dysphoria than do probationers of either type. Non-EM parolees are intermediate between these two groupings. Electronic monitoring, along with the offender's age and type of offense, had an effect on posttest BDI scores that was statistically discernible from zero. The effect of EM in this context is suspected to be attributable to the fact that EM allows convicts an earlier release from institutional custody than would normally be expected. Thus, members of this sub-group feel less restricted and community supervision does not lead to dysphoria as quickly among them.

Control scale posttests were significantly lower for both groups of parolees than for the probationers. This seems best attributed to the fact that parolees tend to have weaker family ties as a result of incarceration and are a less controllable group as a result of their relatively higher level of criminal involvement. Parolees on EM reported significantly less conflict on the posttest than any other group. Conflict post tests follow much the same pattern but no distinctions between EM and non-EM parolees can be made with regard to this variable.

Regression analysis indicated that BDI posttest scores, employment status, and EM supervision had significant effects on posttest conflict scores. The direct and positive effect of BDI scores on familial conflict is not surprising but these data do not allow speculation as to whether dysphoria is a cause or an effect of conflict. The association of the offender's employment status with conflict in the home is difficult to explain. Indeed, quite the opposite direction was expected for these variables. It may be that the more an offender works, the more power he/she expects within the family. Since offenders frequently have relational problems, such expectations could, in the context of a history that includes direct or indirect abuse of family members and/or responsibilities by the offender, be conflict-producing. The impact of EM on reported perceptions of family conflict is noteworthy in this context since the analysis indicates that the presence of EM is associated with low levels of friction within the family. Because this relationship did not attain significance when pretest data were analyzed, the data suggests that EM may have a positive effect in this regard.

The most crucial analyses are those concerning differences between pretest and posttest scores since these changes in subjects' perceptions reflect the impact of EM supervision. Changes in BDI scores were the first to be analyzed. As in earlier analyses, EM parolees were significantly less dysphoric than probationers on either type of supervision. Regression indicated that the offender's age and educational level were significant predictors of changes in dysphoria. Younger and less-well educated offenders were more likely to report increases in dysphoria over the study period than were older or better educated offenders. Younger offenders are less likely to have encountered the criminal justice system and tend to have fewer responsibilities than older, more established persons.

Analysis of the changes in conflict scores over the study period indicated that changes in dysphoria, along with the offender's age and marital status, had significant predictive power. Dysphoria is logically related to conflict but, as has been previously mentioned, the causal relationship between these two variables is unclear and may indeed be reciprocal with each contributing to the other. Marriage was found to be directly related to reported increases in conflict. This is thought to be a result of the greater intimacy and investment implied by such unions, relative to other types of relationships. Age was also directly related to increases in conflict scores. The predictive value of age may be due to the realization that much of one's life has been wasted on criminal, or at least deviant, pursuits.

Analysis of control scale scores indicated that only changes in dysphoria and the offender's employment status had effects that were discernible from zero. Both of these relationships were of a direct (i.e., positive) nature. Thus the data indicate that increases in dysphoria are associated with increases in perceived family control and the more regular the offender's employment, the more likely the perception of increased familial control over time. Neither of these findings are especially surprising, particularly in the context of a population of felony offenders.

The final set of analyses was, in fact, the most crucial to the study because of their focus on determinants of successful completion of community supervision. Because of the aforementioned differences between the probationers and parolees these two groups were analyzed separately before the entire sample was examined. Among probationers three factors were found to predict success: (1) decline in perceived familial control as measured by the FES; (2) decline in reported dysphoria as measured by the BDI; and, (3) the presence of EM. It seems apparent that perceptions of family control may be effected by the use of EM in a positive manner. That is, the use of EM constitutes a control mechanism that replaces the family as a monitor of the offender's activities and whereabouts. Thus, when EM is used the imposition of structure upon the offender's life is firmly linked to the decisions of the probation/parole officer rather than a family member. Therefore, the family ceases to operate as the overseer of the offender's movements but the offender is simultaneously forced into a more structured lifestyle by the demands of EM supervision. By relieving the family of some of its control functions, EM facilitates the establishment of more functional patterns in the offenders' lifestyle, and that of the family, thus serving a role that has, at the very least, some rehabilitative potential.

SIGNIFICANT OTHERS

Testing Devices

Each of the significant others completed a Client Demographic Information Form, a pretest for the Control and Conflict subscales for FES, and a pretest BDI. The client Demographic Information Form was used to collect and identify the following information: (1) the name of the significant other; (2) the agency having jurisdiction over the offender; (3) the county having jurisdiction over the offender; (4) the offender's specific type of supervisory program; (5) the general significant other's socio-demographic characteristics; (6) the offense committed by the offender; (7) an abbreviated criminal history of the offender; (8) an abbreviated substance abuse history of the significant other; and, (9) an abbreviated family environmental history of the significant other.

Socio-Demographic and Added Characteristics of the Subjects

There were a total of 29 significant others that participated in this study. The majority (60%) of these subjects were between the ages of 22 to 35, and 51.7% were nonwhite. Slightly more (58.6%) were males than females (41.4), and 56.7% had not completed high school. More (37.9%) of the subjects were married than single (34.5%), while 27.6% were either separated, divorced, or widowed. Forty-eight point two percent (48.2%) had full time employment and 14.8% were employed part time. Of those for which the type of employment could be identified, 84.6% worked at what would normally be classified as blue collar jobs. Sixty-eight point nine percent (68.9%) stated that they lived in a 3 or 4 member family household with 100% having at least one child living with them. Only 6.9% of the significant others claimed to be living with more than two children.

The offense history of the offenders of the significant others ranged from property crimes, which was the highest category (68.8%), to substance abuse crimes (25%), to crimes against a person (6.2%).

The significant others' alcohol and drug abuse or use histories in regard to their own usage prior to their offenders' arrest indicated that 67.8% abstained from both alcohol or drugs; 17.9% used both alcohol and drugs socially; 10.7% only used drugs socially; and only 3.6% identified themselves as serious abusers of both alcohol and drugs. The survey indicated a decrease in their current usage over that prior to their offenders' arrest. Eighty-nine point three percent (89.3%) claimed to be now abstaining from both alcohol and drugs, with the remaining 10.7% stating that they used both substances socially. None of these persons claimed to be a serious abuser of either substance. The vast majority (93.1%) stated that they had a good relationship with their families.

The significant others were subsequently divided into two groups. One group, significant others of offenders on EM (hereafter referred to as EM significant others), represented 62% of the total sample while the other group, significant others of offenders not on EM (hereafter referred to as non-EM significant others), represented the remaining 38% of the total sample.

In both groups the majority of subjects were found to be between the ages of 22 and 35 (61.4% for EM significant others and 63.7% for non-EM significant others). The EM group contained 72.2% males whereas the non-EM group contained only 36.4%. There were more non-whites than whites in both groups (61.1% for EM significant others and 63.6% for non-EM significant others).

Each group contained about the same number of married subjects (EM group 38.9% and non-EM group 37.9%). They also had approximately the same educational levels (EM group had 55.6% with less than a high school education and the non-EM group had 56.7%). The overall employment patterns for both groups were similar; however, there was a difference between groups for full and part time employment. Twenty-seven point three percent (27.3%) of the non-EM group were employed full time while only 6.3% of the EM group were, and 62.4% of the EM group held part time jobs while only 27.2% of the non-EM group did. Both groups had approximately the same number who were unemployed (45.5% for the non-EM group and 31.3% for the EM group). For those whose type of employment could be established, 74.9% of the non-EM group and 88.8% of the EM group held what would normally be classified as "blue collar" jobs.

Both the EM and non EM groups lived predominately in three or four member family households (66.7% and 72.8 respectively). All (100%) members of both groups lived with at least one child. Also, all (100%) of the non-EM households contained less than three children, whereas 11.2% of the EM households contained three or more children. The histories of offenses committed by the significant others' offenders had a somewhat similar pattern: property offenses accounted for 72.7% of the offenses in the EM group, and for 60% of the offenses for the non-EM group;   substance abuse offenses for the EM group totaled 18.2%, whereas it accounted for 40% of the non-EM group; and, 9.1% of crimes against a person were noted for the EM group compared to 0.0% for the non-EM group.

Both groups had approximately the same alcohol and drug abuse or use histories concerning their own usage prior to their offenders' arrest. The data suggested that 80% of the non-EM group and 61.1% of the EM group abstained from both alcohol and drugs; 10% of the non-EM group claimed to use only drugs socially as did 11.1% of the EM group; 10% of the non-EM group and 22.1% of the EM group reported using both alcohol and drugs socially. None (0.0%) of the non-EM group claimed to seriously abuse either drugs or alcohol; however, 5.6% of the EM group claimed serious abuse of drugs or alcohol. The survey indicated a decrease in both groups in terms of current usage compared to their usage prior to their offenders' arrest: 100% of the non-EM and 83.3% of the EM group claimed to be abstaining from both alcohol and drugs. Sixteen point seven percent (16.7%) of the EM group indicated that they currently were using both alcohol and drugs socially.

There was a slight difference between the two groups regarding how they viewed their family relationships. All (100%) of the non-EM group indicated that they had good family relationships, whereas 11.2% of the EM group did not feel that they had good family relationships.

ANALYSIS

Due to the relatively small sample of significant others, Pearson Product-Moment Correlations (Pearson's r) and t tests were used to test the significance of the relationships existing between the socio-demographic, psychometric, and background variables for the available data. The matrices of correlation coefficients for the socio-demographic variables (age, race, sex, family, employment, marriage, education, household, adults, and children) indicate that only four of the variables were significantly correlated at the 0.01 level. The correlation between subjects' level of education and the type of offense (r = -.4770) was significant. The number of adults in these households was also closely related to the total number of persons living in households as could logically be expected (r = .5354). However, the correlation coefficients for these two pairs of variables indicate that the relationships are only moderate at best. Generally, only correlation coefficients that are greater than 0.70, and that reach statistical significance at the .05 or .01 levels of significance, are interpreted as having a dependable relationship with each other. In short, our interpretation of the correlation coefficients across all of the demographic variables is that no strong relationship exists between any of the variables with respect to the significant others.

The sample of significant others was next divided into two groups: those associated with offenders who were on electronic monitoring and those associated with offenders who were not on EM. A series of t-tests were then employed to test for significant differences between the means scores of these two groups on the conflict and control subscales of the FES. A t-test was also used to determine if differences in mean levels of dysphoria as determined by the BDI were statistically discernible between these two groups of subjects. Neither of these t-tests revealed statistically significant differences between the EM and non-EM groups: The t level equaled 0.23 (P=0.83) for the two groups on dysphoria (EM group mean score=1.24, non-EM group mean=1.30); t equaled 0.33 (P=0.71) for the two groups on family conflict (EM group mean score=2.15, non-EM group mean=2.38); and t equaled 0.64 (P=0.56) for the two groups on family control (EM group mean score=5.41, non-EM group mean=5.73).

In essence, no discernible differences appear to exist between EM and non-EM family environments as perceived by significant others of offenders residing with them, nor does there appear to be any discernable difference in the level of dysphoria between significant others of EM and non-EM offenders. In summary, although the extremely small t values found indicate that no such relationships exist, this conclusion cannot be sustained in this analysis because of the small sample size used.

NOTES

1.   Richard C. Grinter. Electronic Monitoring of Serious Offenders in Texas, Journal of Offender Monitoring, 2 (4): 1-14, 1989.

2.   Delbert Miller. Hollingshead's Two Factor Index of Social Position, in Delbert Miller (ed.), Handbook of Research Design and Social Measurement (3rd ed.) (New York: David McKay Co., 1977).

3.   Rudolf Moos and B. Moos. Family Environment Scale Manual (2nd ed.) (Palo Alto, CA: Consulting Psychologists Press, 1986).

4.   J. Ford, M. Bashford, and K. DeWitt. Prediction of Outcome in Marital Communication Training: An Empirical Investigation (Van Nuys, CA: San Fernando Community Mental Health Center, 1979).

5.   P. Boss. A Clarification of the Concept of Psychological-Father Presence in Families Experiencing Ambiguity of Boundary, Journal of Marriage and the Family, 36: 141-151, 1977.

6.   Marija J. Norusis. Introductory Statistics Guide: SPSSx (New York: McGraw-Hill, 1983).

CHAPTER 9

CRITICAL ISSUES IN THE FUTURE FOR ELECTRONIC
MONITORING PROGRAMS

INTRODUCTION

The issues which were first raised in print when electronic monitoring (EM) emerged as a realistic option are still problematic. Although considerable experience with the process has been gained, current proponents, opponents and the undecided still debate or discuss most of the same queries that were raised initially. Any predictions for future directions of EM must respond to these considerations. The authors believe that the responses must be made within the context or reality of current alternatives and options. Such predictions must acknowledge the importance of an ideal system, but must be both bold and rigorous in evaluating the state of the criminal justice system in its progress toward an "ideal model".

One of the key early concerns with such programs focused upon some general ethical and moral perspectives regarding electronic monitoring and house arrest. The idealists pushed the potential outcome of such monitoring to an ultimate extreme, culminating in the implanting of various electronic devices in the offender's body or brain; or proposed some similar scenario in which some form of electronic technology would be used to guarantee that former and potential offenders would be deterred from criminal behavior. On the other hand, other idealists proposed models of EM that implied total freedom, maturity, self-actualization and the absence of external controls. Because of this group, the potential for electronic monitoring was characterized as, minimally, dangerous, if not outright evil and immoral. Many of us start from such morally and ethically idealist positions and must ultimately resolve reservations created by such ideals before we can approve such programs. However, even the most moral of us are confronted with the fact that not just electronic monitoring, but all responses to criminal justice programs, practices and organizations need to be considered within the existing political climate, the "real world", where the ideal is just that, an ideal. In truth, it is a world of selecting among alternatives, and either perceiving such choices as predicated upon the best possible good (best outcome available) to be obtained, or choosing the better of imperfect alternatives or options.

Specifically, when comparing electronic monitoring or house arrest with the alternatives of a jail, or a medium or maximum security facility, electronic monitoring seems a higher moral choice. This presumes that the clients are individuals who would have been institutionalized as opposed to having been assigned traditional probation. However, this must be evaluated in the light of offenders who have long histories of offenses prior to first probation, and must be weighted against the possibility of further criminal activity if offenders are not placed under surveillance at early stages. Ethical and moral issues, legal rights, and concerns about surveillance and invasion of privacy must be weighed in the balance against victimization, a safe and secure society, and the ultimate good for the offenders themselves.

There is no question that electronic monitoring has significant potential for harmful and dangerous uses, particularly with respect to freedom, human dignity, intrusiveness and social control. But, the same evaluation is equally applicable to almost all other types of criminal justice programs and procedures, including any use of computerization of criminal records. All such programs and procedures must be weighed in the context of the value of each of our freedoms and the freedom of each of us with respect to any potentially dangerous situations that might emerge if such programs and procedures are not used.

LEGAL ISSUES

With reference to legal issues, it needs to be underscored that many of the anticipated legal challenges to the process never materialized. That is not to say that all of the legal opinions have been rendered or that the legal scholars have returned their final verdict. Thus far, the programs have withstood legal scrutiny and challenges. Perhaps this reflects the true merits of the procedures, as compared with alternatives, in the view of offenders. This is not to overlook information that suggests that some inmates, given the opportunity, choose incarceration instead of electronic monitoring and house arrest. An important consideration with respect to the last point is that the situations are rather limited in which courts permit offenders to select or reject certain punishment alternatives. Such strategies have been used to avoid problems with the Fifth Amendment. The assumption is that if the offender is not coerced, then this is not a cruel and unusual punishment, or in violation of other rights. So far, no judges have ruled that electronic monitoring or house arrest violates the rights of other members of the offender's family. Also, it should be noted that the judiciary have not found that probation violates the rights of the offender's family. In having offenders at home, dangers exist from violent offenders and from offenders who are spouse abusers, child abusers or sexual aggressors. This has important implications for other family members with respect to the potential for violating their rights. In comparison, probation is not generally scrutinized with respect to the violation of the rights of other family members. But it is true that precautions are usually taken to probate only the most appropriate individuals. One would anticipate the same kind of caution and rational behavior with respect to electronic monitoring and house arrest. It could be posited that corrections personnel will take considerable caution to prevent using the programs with inappropriate offenders or in family situations which are considerably problematic.

The significant point is that any one specific punishment response has certain ramifications that have the potential to lead to legal recourse. Most do not culminate in such proceedings. This is particularly true of those which more closely approximate the goal of humane treatment of all concerned, if safeguards are provided and if monitoring is on-going.

TECHNICAL EQUIPMENT CONSIDERATIONS

The equipment is available. There is a considerable array designed for very specific circumstances and programs. As could be anticipated, it is much improved over the earliest equipment. There is, however, still considerable probability of mechanical problems or failures. However, a similar analysis might be made of a great number of other offender programs and monitoring strategies, including human and electronic or technical components. Even the best probation officer is prone to human error. It is possible that such errors are no more likely to be discovered or corrected any more quickly when humans are operating these system compared to systems not using human operators.

There have been the typical mechanical problems. These have included problems with the radio signals, interference from other electronic sources, transmission problems, false alarms and failure in the monitors to indicate problems with the probationer. Offenders have damaged, and or removed equipment and disappeared, or committed additional crimes. In the same vein, equipment and procedures fail in other criminal justice programs as well. Even in the newest and most modern jail construction, technical difficulties can occur which pose the risk of harm to correctional personnel or escape of the offender. The point is, there is a diversity of equipment available with high levels of performance which enhance the high probability of success for electronic monitoring and house arrest programs. And, the technical reliability of the equipment is improving.

A criminal justice organization which is considering the use of such equipment needs to detail the goals for which the equipment would be used, to outline the program strategies and processes to be employed, and, finally, to select the equipment which best satisfies these needs or requirements. This should, of course, be done in consultation with the providers of such equipment. Issues such as who will monitor the equipment can be determined with respect to the goals and strategies for the programs. Debates concerning whether probation officers will, or will not, monitor equipment twenty-four hours a day, seven days a week, will be resolved through personnel considerations, just as they have always been answered with respect to innovations or changes in any program. Without question, such changes may increase or decrease morale. However, the same is true in relation to other employment situations. In short, if EM proves to be an effective means for monitoring offenders, or is equal to other means, then it should be used. Such problems, as they arise, can be approached through in-service workshops and other personnel programs, which are useful in re-orienting or re-training personnel.

DESIGN, STRUCTURE AND ORGANIZATIONAL ISSUES

Many of the issues related to program design, structure, organization and implementation of EM programs are now standard operating procedures. For example, with regard to each of these categories, the motivation for adopting the system and the goals of the system determine much of the structure. Any innovation, change or new program policy necessitates attention to these issues. In the actual process, key actors must be involved from the inception and throughout the planning, implementation, maintenance and evaluation steps in the process. Electronic monitoring programs must be adapted to specific communities, departments and needs. Considerable communication is required to elicit the support of the community and significant decision makers and participants. Organizational resources must be directed toward communication with and education of these individuals and groups.

Specifically, agency and staff personnel must be fully involved from the earliest stages and throughout the entire process. The most important external persons or change agents must be included. The program director is the significant and pivotal factor in the success or failure of the program. Almost equally important is the support of the program staff. Other key issues are comparable to those of similar forms of organizations and programs. Decisions will need to be made with respect to particular roles and role expectations. It is not as though such programs are starting without existing traditional probation programs already in place. Yet, the writers noted in their contacts with the departments using EM that much of the early discussions of these programs occurred as though no such background information or existing structures were already in place. The traditional probation program provides the philosophy, structure, goals and personnel into which EM programs can be integrated.

An analysis will need to be made with respect to the characteristics of the local probation programs in order to detail tasks and assignments. A thorough review will need to be made so as to establish operating procedures. For example, attention needs to be given to such issues as: the specific individuals who will monitor the computer operation, who reads the printouts, who interprets the printouts and who responds if the monitoring process reveals a problem with one of the clients. Other considerations will include issues of cost. Exactly how will the program be funded and how will it interface with other programs? Specific strategies will need to be developed for the overall integration of the EM program with other programs in the probation department. Issues such as length of sentences on the equipment, extent of control of the equipment and contract monitoring versus voluntary monitoring or department monitoring will need to be resolved.

The important point here is that these are the ongoing types of decisions that are being made on a continuing basis by probation departments with respect to all programs. Again, much of the conversation or discussion regarding electronic monitoring and or house arrest has been carried on as though these programs would be occurring in a vacuum. In fact, it is critically important to realize that they are not and that they are just one facet of a very complex set of programs administered by departments of probation on a daily basis. Any decisions made regarding electronic monitoring and house arrest will reflect overall goals, funding and personnel issues which also guide other programs.

Thus, much of the discussion focusing upon the need to redefine probation as a result of electronic monitoring, or to move from a model of counseling to surveillance, simply are not valid. Electronic monitoring is an additional and effective tool that should be used with many of the other programs in traditional probation. This technology actually has potential to enhance other traditional programs and possibly make them more effective, efficient and successful for offenders, all other citizens, and society.

In fact, introduction of such technology may require a reassessment of the current strategies any department is using with respect to deployment of probation officers, use of their time, styles of interaction or overall approaches to supervision. This can be a very positive process in itself. Again, it is a process with which most probation departments are familiar as innovations, new state regulations or new programs are introduced. Thus, any chief of probation will need to realize the importance of adaptation in any organization and the dangers attendant upon stagnation or refusal to adopt new technologies. Likewise, the most successful heads quickly learn the importance of goal attainment, including long range planning, goal setting and evaluation. It is almost impossible not to deal with such issues and survive in state and county governments. Heads of probation have shown particularly creative and ingenious means of marshalling the resources to maintain and deliver their programs. In addition, most directors of probation are acutely aware of the importance of integration within their departments. They have experienced the need to integrate state expectations with local and county expectations and to integrate new and old programs, new and old personnel, new and old state regulations and new and old budget and funding patterns. Finally, chiefs of probation and parole have demonstrated some of their greatest skills and abilities in meeting the expectations of local communities, county expectations and the requirements of local, county and state politicians. Most have an operational pattern that demonstrates their awareness of hidden expectations and needs in their roles and organizations. Certainly, most are conscious of the need for the management of stress which is attendant upon the adoption of any innovation, such as EM, and have demonstrated particular skills in managing tensions in an all too frequent atmosphere of highly politicized structures.

ECONOMIC ISSUES

Aside from the major goal of punishment of the offender, the second most important goal of the United States criminal justice system appears to be that of "least cost" corrections. One of the most touted goals of electronic monitoring and house arrest was that it would reduce prison incarceration and population; thus, ultimately reducing correctional costs. The current guiding principle for criminal justice funding seems to be the amount of taxation the citizens are willing to tolerate, the number of police departments and officers they are willing to fund, the number of courts and personnel they are willing to underwrite and the number of prisons and probation departments they are willing to bear. For the corrections component this translates into how many new prisons can be built, the current bed census in the prison system and the specific number of inmates who need to be released in order to make room for the most recently remanded offenders. This kind of short term, cost-benefit economic thinking is in vogue today.

Significantly, few criminal justice professionals and little of the criminal justice literature moves beyond the economic costs on other than a short term basis.

Seldom does one hear or read discussions about the long term costs of crime and delinquency in our society or approaches to policy which calculate alternative uses of monies to avoid higher law enforcement, legal and correctional costs. For example, one could compare, in economic terms, the cost to our society for law enforcement, the judiciary, and corrections, compared to the cost of programs for early, positive human development including, appropriate prefertility programs (that is the significance of creating a pregnancy), preparenting education, parenting education programs, appropriate pre- and post- natal care, recreation opportunities for all children and youth, appropriate day care, preschools and after school care, and the highest quality primary, secondary and higher education opportunities.

It is also important to consider marginal costs. This concept means that the cost of a particular sub-program should be compared with the total cost structure of an entire program. This is a viable way to compare EM programs with other programs within probation departments. This would be particularly relevant in considerations of adopting or eliminating a particularly beneficial program in which the cost was really inconsequential or minor. With respect to the issue of marginal costs, corrections personnel are aware of "sunk costs" in a prison system. In other words, we already have the land and the structures, thus, any correctional system we design needs to use these facilities. Such sunk costs in facilities and personnel always make it more difficult to develop innovations in programs. However, even sunk costs could be a part of the economic calculation the authors are suggesting here.

Criminal justice professionals tend to concentrate upon costs and specifically, short term costs. It needs to be underscored that one can always differentiate human costs from monetary costs. It is argued by the authors that such human costs ultimately can be considered marginal costs in criminal justice and society when compared to the long term costs for neglecting them. Neglect of human costs are attended by heavy monetary, social, psychological, ethical and moral costs.

The decision to use electronic monitoring ought not to predicated upon its cost savings, or rejected if it will not save any money, or if it appears too costly. The issue should be framed in this way: how does it contribute to the overall goal of the criminal justice system, including a safe, secure, moral and positive society?

There are two additional points which need to be discussed when considering economic issues: the concept of "net widening", and the impact of EM upon victims and upon the families or significant others of offenders. Concerning net widening, the greatest unknown factor is whether these programs will widen the criminal justice net by assigning people to them who would, under usual circumstances, be placed on traditional probation or be directed into alternative programs. There is genuine concern that such net widening will occur and, indeed, has already occurred. Thus, if individuals are assigned to electronic monitoring who would ordinarily be incarcerated, and if this system ultimately leads to fewer incarcerations, then costs might be reduced. However, it has been suggested that even here, the real reduction in costs is only if you do not build new facilities, that is, you already have a sunk cost in the original facilities. The cost of operating these is a fairly constant cost, whatever the number of occupants. In addition, if you net widen by simply sending the same number of people to prison, and increasing the number of people you monitor outside of prison, then you actually increase the criminal justice system costs. Likewise, if you put people on electronic monitoring who fail on that system, particularly with respect to technical violations, then you have that cost, the reprocessing cost and the add on cost of prison.

There is no question that net widening has occurred and will continue to accompany these programs. Net widening is not the central issue here. At issue is the intent of the program. That is, how best to accomplish the goals and determining who can best benefit from these programs. These must be factored into the long term benefits to victims, society and offenders. There is genuine possibility that early use of electronic monitoring along with other alternative programs may reduce the cost to individuals and society of offender behavior.   A second   consideration concerns the safety and security of the victim and other members of society, including the families and significant others of the offenders. It is important to note that most citizens are unaware of these programs, just as they are unaware of most of the programs administered by probation departments. Responses have been positive in situations in which citizens and leaders of the community have become aware of these programs. Managers of such programs need to develop and maintain citizen support. This might include discussions with a citizens advisory board concerning the safety and security issues, screening and client selection procedures, and the concept of a reasonable right to know. The cost of such programs and funding procedures might also be discussed with such a board. Attempts might be made to inform the public with respect to these last two issues.

Electronic monitoring also has a special significance for the families of offenders, especially if the offender has a history of violence to an individual, family violence, spouse battering, or child abuse and neglect. The concern, of course, centers on the possibility of a continuation of such offenses. Furthermore, while the offender might be less restricted than if he/she were in prison, the lives of the families of such offenders might be more limited, altered and their privacy circumscribed. Ironically, family members may, in a sense, be serving the sentence along with the offender. An example of this has been the use of telephones to transmit the radio frequency from the computer. In such cases, conversations in which families members might be engaged can actually be interrupted momentarily for the transmission signal.

It would appear, however, that the benefits for families have thus far considerably outweighed any of these kinds of negative effects. In other words, these concerns simply have not seemed significant in the real world of the offender families. The benefits of sustaining some continuity of the family, possibilities of employment, presence of another adult to provide at least minimal assistance with children, and avoidance of the stigma of having a family member sent to prison, seem to have been significantly more important than the risks to safety, security and privacy. This last issue is a ripe topic for social science research efforts.

COUNSELING VERSUS SURVEILLANCE

Considerable discussion with respect to electronic monitoring and house arrest has focused upon a false dichotomy regarding whether such programs will be rehabilitative or supervisory. It is the opinion of the authors that this is a fallacious argument, much as that of the keeper versus counselor argument with respect to prison guards. Both roles can be accomplished in each setting. That is not to suggest that both roles in each situation are not difficult tasks. Without question, in each situation, the counseling role is most difficult.

But, it is important to underscore that supervision is not mutually exclusive with respect to the goals of therapy. The same concept can be reversed with respect to therapy. Such programs can be, and have already been, complementary. The same point can be made with respect to various other programs in criminal justice or rehabilitation which frequently involve dual roles which are sometimes minimally in conflict and in other cases quite contradictory in nature. Still, individuals are asked to assume both roles, or the roles are divided between two or more individuals. As with other programs, the solution lies in identifying goals, motivating the clients, integrating them into the program, monitoring their participation, and, finally, evaluating the outcomes of their participation in the program.

One of the factors that makes the counselor/surveillance and rehabilitation/surveillance arguments moot is the opportunity for continuous monitoring by computers and third party contractors, thus freeing the probation officer to concentrate his or her efforts in a counseling framework. It cannot be emphasized too strongly that roles of counseling and surveillance are ideal types. Within the criminal justice system, it has never been an either/or perspective with respect to these practices. Traditional probation officers or intensive probation supervisors have had to balance the roles of rehabilitation and counseling with their roles as monitors and gatekeepers regarding violations and revocation of parole.

In determining the levels of success of these programs, some measure of least restrictive conditions should be employed. Any discussion of measures of success is particularly pertinent to the electronic monitoring programs, since too rigid measures of success are a set up for failure. It has been the experience of the authors that much more rigid measures of success are usually applied to innovative programs than to programs which fit the traditional adversarial, punishment and control models in the criminal justice system. A consistent problem in the criminal justice system, and particularly with therapeutic models for individual behavior change, is that they are given limited opportunity of demonstrating their strength. The field of corrections is replete with failed models for rehabilitating offenders. Yet, a considerable number of years has been provided to demonstrate the futility of the penal model and still it is advocated and tolerated. Human and social change requires significant numbers of years, perhaps 25 to 75 years, to make differences in human and social problems that have been an equal number of years in the making. They certainly deserve every right to be given as great an opportunity of failure as the prison system. While criminal justice professionals might differ with respect as to whether anything can change serious adult offenders, there are few such professionals claiming that the prison has the potential to engender such changes. Electronic monitoring, on the other hand, when used in concert with other community corrections approaches, demonstrates considerable promise to make such significant changes.

SELECTION CRITERIA AND SCREENING

The guiding principle with respect to selection for EM programs has been that of the risk to the safety and security of individuals, groups and society at large. Certainly, any issue of reasonably foreseen risk should be a guiding factor for heads of probation in developing selection and screening criteria. Unfortunately, a second guiding principle has usually been to demonstrate the punitiveness of the programs as a reaction to public and political pressures for punishment and deterrence instead of being able to focus upon the genuine correctional possibilities of EM as an innovation.

Interestingly enough, there is some evidence to suggest that offenders may, in fact, consider electronic monitoring as too restrictive, or too punitive. In some situations, when offenders have been given options, they have elected traditional incarceration instead of EM. Such decisions may reflect a variety of factors, including the anticipation that less "real time" would be spent under surveillance in a prison than on electronic monitoring in the community or at home. It is true that many individuals may find confinement to the home more restrictive, problematic or punitive than incarceration. Still, the courts are not in the habit of making decisions with respect to adjudication to specific facilities upon the preference of the offender. It is interesting that criminal justice professionals would assume that the courts should or would start such selection of adjudicatory assignment with electronic monitoring. The one caveat is, of course, the consideration as to whether such a program, freely chosen, can be an infringement of the offenders rights and freedoms, including the right to privacy.

Early recommendations regarding criteria and selection for offenders on electronic monitoring stressed the importance of careful and responsible screening. In practice, these programs have been extensively directed toward first time offenders, nonviolent offenders, and property offenders. These are important considerations. Certainly, every attention should be made to identify variables that might be predictive of success on electronic monitoring, just as is done with other probation programs and with parole. In every case, the probable success, failure and potential risk of each individual offender needs to be weighed with respect to that specific individual. A part of this consideration would need to include the nature of the offense prior to plea bargaining. Such information is difficult to factor into the decisions given the fact of charging an offender with a higher offense, or with a long series of offenses, even when all concerned are aware the higher charge will not stand up in court, or that many of the charges will be dropped.

Research by the authors and in the criminal justice field suggests that a high degree of success for electronic monitoring of offenders exists when the technology has been used with such low risk offenders as the first time offender, nonviolent property offenders and with other types of nonviolent offenders. However, research attention should be increasingly directed toward evaluating carefully selected serious offenders placed on EM. Without question, this must be done with extreme caution. However, it must be initiated if the full potential of EM is to be ascertained. Otherwise, its utility will be extremely limited and its potential for net widening greater.

No doubt, there are some offenses and some offenders for whom these monitoring programs are inappropriate. Although many murderers might be excellent candidates for probation and electronic monitoring, societal and political responses might make it impossible to use this technology with them.

Other behaviors which represent life styles which have been suggested as lower order probabilities for success include racketeering, extortion and murder for hire. Some advocates of electronic monitoring caution against using the programs with a broad category of offenders. These include offenders with a history of violence, weapons offenses, long prison terms, domestic violence, chronic drug and alcohol abuse, and those with serious psychological problems. However, since such offenders will, in fact, be released at some point, appropriately screened offenders, even in these categories, might be viable candidates who would benefit from such programs. Since such individuals will be released, the programs could be evaluated either for use with probation or parole. Undeniably, its use with parole would reflect a conscious widening of the criminal justice net. However, it would be one means of attempting to reduce recidivism.

Another use which has been little discussed, if at all, also widens the net and may again be perceived as a preventative measure, is the potential of the use of electronic monitoring in prisons to reduce complications for taking random prison census. With a sophisticated monitoring system, the location and specific identity of each inmate would be instantly available.

Use of electronic monitoring with respect to a wide variety of offenders, and chronic drug and or alcohol use, coupled with other components of probation, might be very effective with such offenders. Again, at some point, these offenders will be out of incarceration. With very careful screening, it may be beneficial for some offenders to learn to live in a family context. Electronic monitoring may provide that possibility. Such programs might be used in the same situations with those on parole. It should be emphasized that such programs have already been implemented with each of these groups. For example, some of the very earliest successes have been with DWIs. Programs have already been implemented for use in family violence and domestic violence situations. Once more, these programs underscore the importance of linking counseling/rehabilitation with electronic monitoring.

There are other factors which might be factored into the screening process which are more specifically related to the personality and social characteristics of the offender. In particular, how the offender perceives his/her responsibility for the criminal behavior, his or her ability to conceptualize the harm done by the act to individuals and the society, the nature of support provided by the home environment and from significant others, and the spirit of cooperation or willingness to become involved in a process of counseling/rehabilitation linked with electronic monitoring.

The writers suggest that any or all of these factors might be used in the selection and screening process. Considerable flexibility needs to be used in establishing the criteria for selection for electronic monitoring. The screening process also needs to provide flexibility even with respect to the offense itself. That is, before any particular offenses are ruled out for EM, the screening process should provide for the inclusion of offenses which political, legal, and social circumstances would not otherwise exclude, and for which the criteria for reasonable public safety and security would be met. This equation would be balanced by a realistic assessment about how the rehabilitative potential in the use of EM might make a difference for the particular offender.

Finally, with respect to potential clients, the authors contend that these programs have not yet begun to be utilized to their fullest benefit or effect with juveniles. Given that these uses would be a conscious net widening, and that a variety of other problems would be attendant with such use, it still can be argued that it has considerable humane potential for monitoring youth whose parents cannot or will not monitor them.

SUMMARY AND CONCLUSIONS

Electronic monitoring provides one of those rare circumstances in which a specific program provides a realistic opportunity to significantly change the direction of major criminal justice organizations and the social interactions associated with them. The threat to privacy, increases in the intensity of surveillance (the serious, sophisticated, and additive involvement in surveillance) and the expanded intensity of monitoring (the increased numbers of persons monitored), is real. Yet, it also offers a genuine opportunity of significantly decreasing the use of incarceration.

A careful balance will need to be created. In the opinion of the authors, the destructive capacity of incarceration and institutionalization far outweigh the dangers and risks of electronic monitoring. It is not as though many of the concerns and risks attached to electronic monitoring are not already a reality in our current criminal justice system and, particularly, the jail and prison system. However, electronic monitoring may provide an opportunity to break the dangerous and destructive psychopathological socialization patterns fostered within prison systems. In short, there is every possibility that an Orwellian world may be embodied in electronic monitoring, but then there is a darker world of the jail and prison system that may far outweigh that contingency.